PUFF
LEGEND OF THE

In the aftermath of the War... a pleasant land celebrating a new ruler. For the inhabitants of the remote village of Karnstein, however, it is a place of soul-rending fear! Five ghostly figures have stepped out of an ancient legend and into the light of day. The Shadow Warriors are riding, hunting down human beings and putting them to the sword. But why?

YOU are a veteran of the wars, wandering the land in search of adventure, when you are hired to solve the mystery of the Shadow Warriors. What you discover will affect the life of everyone in the Old World, not least your own.

Two dice, a pencil and an eraser are all you need to embark on this heart-stopping adventure, which is complete with its own elaborate combat system and a score sheet to record your progress.

Many dangers lie ahead of you, and your success is by no means certain. Adversaries from your darkest nightmares are ranged against you, and it's up to YOU to decide which route to follow, which dangers to risk and which foes to fight!

Fighting Fantasy Gamebooks

1. THE WARLOCK OF FIRETOP MOUNTAIN
2. THE CITADEL OF CHAOS
3. THE FOREST OF DOOM
4. STARSHIP TRAVELLER
5. CITY OF THIEVES
6. DEATHTRAP DUNGEON
7. ISLAND OF THE LIZARD KING
8. SCORPION SWAMP
9. CAVERNS OF THE SNOW WITCH
10. HOUSE OF HELL
11. TALISMAN OF DEATH
12. SPACE ASSASSIN
13. FREEWAY FIGHTER
14. TEMPLE OF TERROR
15. THE RINGS OF KETHER
16. SEAS OF BLOOD
17. APPOINTMENT WITH F. E. A. R.
18. REBEL PLANET
19. DEMONS OF THE DEEP
20. SWORD OF THE SAMURAI
21. TRIAL OF CHAMPIONS
22. ROBOT COMMANDO
23. MASKS OF MAYHEM
24. CREATURE OF HAVOC
25. BENEATH NIGHTMARE CASTLE
26. CRYPT OF THE SORCERER
27. STAR STRIDER
28. PHANTOMS OF FEAR
29. MIDNIGHT ROGUE
30. CHASMS OF MALICE
31. BATTLEBLADE WARRIOR
32. SLAVES OF THE ABYSS
33. SKY LORD
34. STEALER OF SOULS
35. DAGGERS OF DARKNESS
36. ARMIES OF DEATH
37. PORTAL OF EVIL
38. VAULT OF THE VAMPIRE
39. FANGS OF FURY
40. DEAD OF NIGHT
41. MASTER OF CHAOS
42. BLACK VEIN PROPHECY
43. THE KEEP OF THE LICH-LORD
44. LEGEND OF THE SHADOW WARRIORS

Steve Jackson's SORCERY!

1. THE SHAMUTANTI HILLS
2. KHARÉ – CITYPORT OF TRAPS
3. THE SEVEN SERPENTS
4. THE CROWN OF KINGS

FIGHTING FANTASY – The Introductory Role-Playing Game
THE RIDDLING REAVER – Four thrilling adventures
THE TROLLTOOTH WARS – A Fighting Fantasy Novel

The Advanced Fighting Fantasy System
OUT OF THE PIT: Fighting Fantasy Monsters
TITAN: The Fighting Fantasy World
DUNGEONEER – An Introduction to the World of Role–Playing Games
BLACKSAND! – More Advanced Fighting Fantasy

Steve Jackson and Ian Livingstone present

LEGEND OF THE SHADOW WARRIORS

Stephen Hand

Illustrated by Martin McKenna

PUFFIN BOOKS

PUFFIN BOOKS

Published by the Penguin Group
27 Wrights Lane, London W8 5TZ, England
Viking Penguin Inc., 40 West 23rd Street, New York, New York 10010, USA
Penguin Books Australia Ltd, Ringwood, Victoria, Australia
Penguin Books Canada Ltd, 2801 John Street, Markham, Ontario, Canada L3R 1B4
Penguin Books (NZ) Ltd, 182–190 Wairau Road, Auckland 10, New Zealand

Penguin Books Ltd, Registered Offices: Harmondsworth, Middlesex, England

First published 1991
1 3 5 7 9 10 8 6 4 2

Concept copyright © Steve Jackson and Ian Livingstone, 1991
Text copyright © Stephen Hand, 1991
Illustrations copyright © Martin McKenna, 1991
Map copyright © Leo Hartas, 1991
All rights reserved

The moral right of the author has been asserted

Filmset in 11/13 pt Monophoto Palatino
Printed in England by Clays Ltd, St Ives plc

Except in the United States of America, this book is sold subject
to the condition that it shall not, by way of trade or otherwise, be lent,
re-sold, hired out, or otherwise circulated without the publisher's
prior consent in any form of binding or cover other than that in which
it is published and without a similar condition including this condition
being imposed on the subsequent purchaser

CONTENTS

HOW TO FIGHT THE CREATURES OF THE OLD WORLD
7

ADVENTURE SHEET
18

BACKGROUND
21

LEGEND OF THE SHADOW WARRIORS
27

*To Josef Hawel whose great kindness
showed me that there are at least
two sides to every big story.*

HOW TO FIGHT THE CREATURES OF THE OLD WORLD

Before embarking on your perilous adventure, you must work out your own strengths and weaknesses; use the *Adventure Sheet* on pages 18–19 to record all the details of your adventure. It will be sensible to make copies of the *Adventure Sheet* for further sorties into this adventure. As well as a copy of the *Adventure Sheet*, you will also need two dice, a pencil and an eraser.

Skill, Stamina and Luck

Roll one die. Add 6 to the number rolled and enter the total in the SKILL box on the *Adventure Sheet*.

Roll two dice. Add 12 to the number rolled and enter the total in the STAMINA box.

Roll one die, add 6 and enter the total in the LUCK box.

For reasons that will be explained below all your scores will change during the adventure. You must keep an accurate record of these scores, and for this reason you are advised to write small in the boxes or to keep an eraser handy. But never rub out your *Initial* scores. As in other *Fighting Fantasy Gamebooks*, although you may be awarded additional SKILL, STAMINA and LUCK points, their totals may never exceed their *Initial* scores, except on those very rare occasions when the text specifically tells you so.

Your SKILL score reflects your expertise in combat, your dexterity and agility. Your STAMINA score reflects how healthy and physically fit you are. Your LUCK score indicates how lucky you are. In all these cases, the higher your score, the better!

Battles

During your adventure you will often encounter hostile creatures which will attack you, and on other occasions you yourself may choose to draw your sword against an enemy you chance across. In some situations you may be given a special option, allowing you to deal with the encounter in an unusual manner; but in most cases you will have to resolve battles as described below.

You will be told your opponent's SKILL and STAMINA scores in the paragraph where you first meet it; enter them in the first vacant Encounter Box on your *Adventure Sheet*. You should also make a note of any special abilities or instructions which are unique to that particular opponent. Then follow this sequence:

1. Roll both dice for your opponent. Add its SKILL score to the total rolled, to find its Attack Strength.

2. Roll both dice for yourself, then add your current SKILL score to find your Attack Strength.

3. If your Attack Strength is higher than your op-

ponent's, you have wounded it: proceed to step 4. If your opponent's Attack Strength is higher than yours, it has wounded you: proceed to step 5. If both Attack Strength totals are the same, you have avoided or parried each other's blows: start a new Attack Round from step 1, above.

4. You have wounded your opponent: subtract 2 points from its STAMINA score. You may use LUCK here to do additional damage to it (see below). Now proceed to step 6.

5. Your opponent has wounded you: subtract 2 points from your STAMINA score. You may use LUCK here to minimize the amount of STAMINA lost (see below).

6. Begin the next Attack Round, starting again at step 1.

This sequence continues until the STAMINA score of either you or your opponent reaches zero, which means death. If your opponent dies, you are free to continue with your adventure. If you die, your quest ends and you must start the adventure all over again by rolling the dice to create a new character.

Special Equipment

During the course of your adventure you may be fortunate enough to get your hands on special weapons and protective armour. If you wield a special weapon in combat, any blows you land on your opponent will do greater damage – your foe will lose more STAMINA than normal; if you enter battle wearing armour, you will be more or less protected from any blows which your opponent lands on you – you will lose fewer points of STAMINA than normal. Instructions covering all these cases are given in the paragraphs where the special equipment is to be found. Any rules concerning special weapons that you read there always take precedence over the rules given in the Battles section, above.

Fighting More Than One Opponent

In some situations you may find yourself facing more than one enemy. Sometimes you will treat them as a single opponent; sometimes you will be able to fight each in turn; and sometimes you will have to fight them all at the same time! If they are treated as a single opponent, the combat is resolved normally. When you are instructed to fight your opponents one at a time, the combat is again resolved normally – except that once you defeat a creature, the next steps forward to fight you! When you find yourself under attack from more than one opponent at the same time, each adversary will make a separate attack on you in the course of each Attack Round, but you can choose which one to fight. Attack your chosen target as in a normal battle. Against any additional opponents you throw for your Attack Strength in the normal way; if your Attack Strength is greater than your opponent's, however, you will not inflict a wound in this instance; you can regard it as if you have parried an incoming blow. If your Attack Strength is lower than your enemy's, however, you will be wounded in the normal way. Of course, you will have to settle the outcome against each additional adversary separately.

Luck

At various times during your adventure, either in battles or when you come across other situations in which you could be either Lucky or Unlucky (details of these are given in the paragraphs themselves), you may use LUCK to make the outcome more favourable to you. But beware! Using LUCK is a risky business and, if you are Unlucky, the results could be disastrous.

The procedure, called *Testing your Luck*, works in the following way: roll two dice. If the number rolled is equal to or less than your current LUCK score, you have been Lucky and the outcome will be in your favour. If the number rolled is higher than your current LUCK score, you have been Unlucky and will be penalized.

Each time you *Test your Luck*, you must subtract 1 point from your current LUCK score. Thus you will soon realize that, the more you rely on your LUCK, the more risky will this procedure become.

Using Luck in Battles

In certain paragraphs you will be told to *Test your Luck*, and you will then find out the consequences of being Lucky or Unlucky. However, in battles, you always have the option of using your LUCK, either to inflict more serious damage on an opponent you have just wounded, or to minimize the effects of a wound you have just received.

If you have just wounded an opponent, you may *Test your Luck* as described above. If you are Lucky, you have inflicted a severe wound; deduct 2 *extra* points from your opponent's STAMINA score. If you are Unlucky, however, your blow only scratches your opponent; and you deduct only 1 point from your opponent's STAMINA (i.e., instead of scoring the normal 2 points of damage, you now score only 1).

Whenever you yourself are wounded in combat, you may *Test your Luck* to try to minimize the wound. If you are Lucky, your opponent's blow only grazes you; deduct only 1 point from your STAMINA. If you are Unlucky, your wound is a serious one and you must deduct 1 *extra* STAMINA point (i.e., deduct a total of 3 points from your own STAMINA).

Remember: you must subtract 1 point from your LUCK score each time you *Test your Luck*.

More About Your Attributes

Skill

Your SKILL score will not change much during the course of your adventure. Occasionally, a paragraph may give instructions to increase or decrease your SKILL score, but it may not exceed its *Initial* value unless you are specifically instructed to the contrary. If you ever have to fight a battle with your bare hands (that is to say, you do not have a weapon to fight with), you must temporarily subtract 1 from your current SKILL score for the duration of the combat.

At various times during your adventure, you will be told to *Test your Skill*. The procedure for this is exactly the same as that for *Testing your Luck*: roll two dice. If the number rolled is equal to or less than your current SKILL score, you have succeeded in your test and the result will go in your favour. If the number rolled is higher than your current SKILL score, you will have failed the test and will have to suffer the consequences. However, unlike *Testing your Luck*, do not subtract 1 point from your SKILL each time you *Test your Skill*.

Stamina

Your STAMINA score will change a lot during your adventure. It will drop as a result of wounds gained through combat, or by falling foul of traps and pitfalls, and it will also drop after you perform any particularly arduous task. If your STAMINA score ever falls to zero, you have been killed and should stop reading the book immediately. Brave adventurers who wish to pursue their quest must roll up a new character and start all over again.

You can restore lost STAMINA by eating meals or Provisions. You start the game with no Provisions, but you will be given the opportunity to obtain food during your adventure. You must keep track of how many meals' worth of Provisions you have by filling in the details in the Provisions box of your *Adventure Sheet*. Each time you eat a meal you may restore up to 4 points of STAMINA, and you must deduct one meal from your Provisions box. You may stop and eat Provisions at any time except when you are engaged in a battle.

Remember, your STAMINA score may never exceed its *Initial* value, so there's no point in eating meals if your STAMINA is already at its maximum.

Luck

Additions to your LUCK score may be awarded in the course of the adventure when you have been particularly lucky or have created your own luck by some action. Details are given in the relevant paragraphs of the book. Remember that, as with SKILL and STAMINA, your LUCK score may never exceed its *Initial* value – unless you are specifically told that it can.

Equipment and Gold

At the beginning of your adventure you have very little equipment that is suitable for a journey of any kind; but you will be given a chance to visit the market at Royal Lendle before embarking on your dangerous quest. During your travels you may also find other useful items which you can take. For now, though, you have only a sword, a backpack and a pouch holding a few Gold Pieces. To find out how many Gold Pieces you have, roll two dice and add 12 to the total rolled. Then note the following items on your *Adventure Sheet*: your sword (in the Weapon box) and your money (in the Gold Pieces box). If later on you should come across any items which you want to take with you, make a note of them in the Equipment box (they are kept in your pack) unless the paragraph tells you otherwise.

Weapons

Though you start the adventure with a sword of gleaming steel, you may get the chance to acquire another weapon. If you take another weapon, you must discard your old one, as you can only ever carry one weapon at a time. To discard a weapon, just erase it from the Weapon box of your *Adventure Sheet*, and then enter the name of the newly acquired weapon in the same box, with a note as to any special instructions that go with it. Once a weapon is discarded, it is lost for ever.

Remember: if you ever have to fight without a weapon, subtract 1 point from your current SKILL score for the duration of the entire battle.

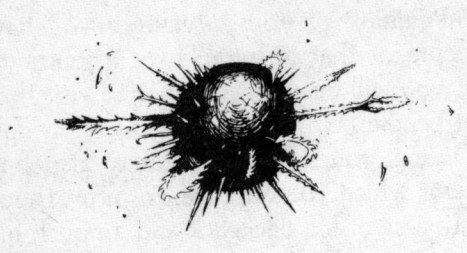

Armour

You start the adventure wearing no armour, but you may be lucky enough to obtain some later on. If you do get your hands on some armour, note it in the Armour box of your *Adventure Sheet* – the paragraph where you find the armour will tell you the type of armour it is. Of course you can wear only one type of armour at any particular time; if you find more and wish to keep it, you will have to discard the armour you are currently wearing. Just erase the old armour from the Armour box of your *Adventure Sheet*, and then enter the name of the new armour, along with any instructions that go with it. Once armour has been discarded, it is gone for ever. You may also discard armour if you quite simply no longer wish to wear it. In such cases, just erase the armour from your *Adventure Sheet*. You may carry out this action at any time, except during a battle.

The various types of armour all work in the same way: they give you some form of protection in battles ... but only for a certain length of time – even the finest Dwarven plate can take only a certain amount of hammering before it starts to buckle. Due to its bulk, armour also hinders your movements, unfortunately.

In the paragraph where you find the armour you will also be told both the total number of hits that the armour can take before it is ruined and exactly how the armour will protect you. Whenever you lose an Attack Round while you are wearing armour, the armour will automatically protect you – whether you want it to or not! As a result, you will lose fewer STAMINA points than normal, and you may even not have to lose any STAMINA at all! However, because the armour will have protected you, you must add 1 to the number of hits that the armour has taken. As soon as the number of hits taken by the armour reaches the total number of hits that it can take, it becomes useless straight away. You may no longer receive the armour's protection and must erase it from the Armour box of your *Adventure Sheet*.

The paragraph in which you find the armour will also tell you to add at least 1 to your dice-rolls whenever you have to *Test your Skill*, thus reducing your chance of success in the test. This penalty is because of the armour's bulk, and it affects you for as long as the armour is included on your *Adventure Sheet*. Wearing armour has no other effect on your SKILL score.

ADVENTURE SHEET

SKILL	STAMINA	LUCK
Initial Skill=	Initial Stamina=	Initial Luck=

WEAPON

PROVISIONS

ARMOUR

EQUIPMENT

GOLD PIECES

NOTES

MONSTER ENCOUNTER BOXES

Skill= *Stamina*=	*Skill*= *Stamina*=	*Skill*= *Stamina*=
Skill= *Stamina*=	*Skill*= *Stamina*=	*Skill*= *Stamina*=
Skill= *Stamina*=	*Skill*= *Stamina*=	*Skill*= *Stamina*=
Skill= *Stamina*=	*Skill*= *Stamina*=	*Skill*= *Stamina*=

*Shadow Warriors
On steeds infernal,
Riding ever faster,
Uprooting tree and breaking stone,
Searching for their Master.*

BACKGROUND

Gallantaria was once the most civilized land on the face of Titan. Its history began when Orjan the Builder halted the great roaming of his tribe, to build a village which he called Lendle. From there, his people spread, building ever more villages, and Lendle itself evolved into a walled city. Orjan's son, Regulus, led the people into a new age of wealth, and forged the eight largest towns into the nation of Gallantaria, with Royal Lendle as its capital. Gallantaria continued to expand and could well have covered the entire Old World, were it not for the fact that it bordered other nations whose peoples also had thoughts of expansion ...

Directly south lay the nation of Femphrey, and to the east the country of Brice. Though initially relations were cordial, the people of Brice grew jealous of Gallantaria's wealth and prepared an invasion. Next, Gallantarian colonies in the Northlands rebelled and sent an army down into their parent country to win their independence, and it did not take long before the nearby nations of Femphrey and Lendleland got caught up in these terrible events. Thus began the War of the Four Kingdoms.

extracts from *Life on Titan*
by Ernst Kandermann

The treacherous Baron Tag led his own monarch into an ambush, he himself plunging a poisoned dagger into King Constain's back. War-torn and leaderless, Gallantaria fell into despair. Fortunately help was at hand in the form of Tantalon, the court magician, who seized the throne 'in the name of the people'. Using a mixture of cunning, wizardry and brilliant strategy, Tantalon brought the war to an end single-handed. Yet, though he exercised the authority of kingship, he did not keep the crown for himself; he was saving it for another.

> excerpt from *Court Essays and Observations:*
> *two decades of royal decorum*
> by Hugo Montpeilier

Aged and weary, Tantalon killed two birds with one stone: at one and the same time he found Constain's successor and righted twelve wrongs by declaring the latter to be tasks which the former had to complete to win the crown. Thus a new blood-line began to rule Gallantaria, Orjan's lineage having ended with the betrayed Constain. Law and order were restored and an unlikely hero became king. Strangely enough, the coronation coincided with Tantalon's passing away; but the wizard's death and the start of a fresh royal dynasty signalled a new era for the nation.

However, Gallantaria was no longer the centre of the Old World. That position had passed to Femphrey, the realm of King Chalanna, who ruled with his magical 'crown of kings'. Chalanna lent this great artefact to the rulers of the other countries, on condition that they join his now mighty Alliance. Indeed, Chalanna's wise and generous leadership has proved to be the sole guiding light, leading us into the next Age of Humanity.

> extract from *Chalanna the Reformer, Vol. III: The Fruitful Years*
> by Matra Sanscreer

Sword For Hire

You are a veteran adventurer, lending your sword-arm to (almost) anybody who makes you the right offer – though it must be said you have no great love for gold, requiring only enough to get by. You seek adventure and excitement for their own sake and look to correct the world's many injustices. Over the years you have fought for many armies and have joined many expeditions into unknown lands. During the War of the Four Kingdoms you fought on the side of Gallantaria, your homeland. Your courage, skill and leadership earned you many decorations and, though you never felt comfortable with it, the rank of captain. When the war ended, you spurned the fame you had gained and took to the road in search of fresh adventures.

Five years on, you are now back in Royal Lendle; but the people who once sang your praises have forgotten you. It's taken only four days for you to become bored with the city so, hopeful of bumping into someone interesting, you decide to take yourself to a tavern named the First Step to slake your thirst. It is highly likely that someone in here will be looking for a person with your particular talents. Indeed, you are on the point of draining your second tankard of Lendale when you feel a frantic tapping on your shoulder and you turn to face a worried-looking man.

Judging by his appearance, you would say that he is a farmer living on the country's borderland. His words tumble out in hurried anxiety. 'Please, Captain, you must help us in Karnstein. Our homes are being ravaged by an unstoppable foe and our people are being cut down like dead wheat. Three of us — that's me, Mendokan, and two of my fellow villagers — have come to the city seeking help, but the authorities won't listen to us. They think we're making it all up. They don't believe that we're being attacked by the Shadow Warriors.'

It cannot be! The Shadow Warriors are merely bogeymen, used by mothers to make their naughty children behave; every Gallantarian child knows the short nursery-rhyme that tells of them.

Before you have time to respond, Mendokan continues. 'No one will help us. Even mercenaries we approached have laughed in our faces. Then, when we heard you were here ... You're our last hope. Will you help us?'

While his words have hardly been a glowing tribute to your skills, you can see that the man is terrified and in dire need of help. You're very doubtful about this Shadow Warrior business, though. It is much more likely that the people of Karnstein are being terrorized by a gang of brigands got up in frightening costumes. Still, you have heard of Karnstein; it's a mere speck of dust on the maps, there's virtually nothing there. What could raiders possibly want from such a place? Perhaps they just enjoy picking on scared, helpless peasants? Whatever the reason, it enrages you to hear of such wanton viciousness. You make up your mind to go to Karnstein on the spot: you'll defend the village and teach these 'Shadow Warriors' a lesson they'll never forget.

Turn to 1.

1

Though he is relieved that you have agreed to help his village, Mendokan now begins to look embarrassed. He says, 'We are only a poor and simple people. All we can pay you is two hundred Gold Pieces and, what is more, the village elders have decreed that you are to be paid after the job is done.' Heigh-ho, such are the times! Still, you won't go back on your word, so you agree to his terms and Mendokan smiles once more in relief. Now he must go and find his friends so that they can prepare to leave for Karnstein; you yourself will have to buy Provisions and other equipment necessary for the journey and your adventure. You shake hands with Mendokan and arrange to meet his party on the Main Trade Route, south of the city, in two hours' time. The farmer then hurries out of the tavern – just as a gaudily dressed fellow strolls in and elbows his way towards you.

This is Bartolph, an infamous gambler; he struts through even the most dangerous parts of the city wearing expensive silks, as a sign of his success at countless gaming tables. 'I haven't seen you in here for some time,' he says with a sly grin. 'Care to try your luck?'

Although you shouldn't be wasting any time here, a win would enable you to buy more equipment and thus prepare you for the road ahead. If you accept Bartolph's challenge, turn to **86**. If you would rather leave, turn to **30**.

2

The leap is not going to be an easy one. *Test your Skill*. If you succeed, turn to **24**; but if you fail, turn to **131**.

3

3

To say that an uneasy silence descends on the bar would be an understatement, but you do your best to ignore the group. If you want to buy a tankard of ale, it will cost you a Gold Piece (cross 1 Gold Piece off your *Adventure Sheet*) and as it goes down you can feel it doing you good (restore 2 STAMINA points). You stand by the bar, listening in on the motley group's conversation. The veterans believe that the Orc is a monk from Femphrey! Either they have been drugged or else the Orc is using a magical disguise. Just then, the Man-Orc walks up to the bar, orders a pint of ale – and then throws it in your face! Anger sends the blood rushing to your cheeks and you turn to face the Orc, who shouts, 'Did you just spill my pint?' Will you attack the Orc (turn to **132**), or try to prove to the others that he *is* an Orc and not a Femphreyan monk (turn to **310**)?

4

Though your evil foe has fallen, he has struck you with a cruel-blade, a magical dagger that inflicts cuts which continue to deepen even after the weapon itself has been withdrawn. The wounds grow and worsen, resulting in a slow and painful death. Fortunately you know the proper treatment for such ill: you must seal the cruel-wounds with heat; only then will they heal normally. If you have a lantern (and oil), you must light it and press its hot glass against your injured flesh (deduct one skin of oil from your *Adventure Sheet*). However, this cure is so painful that it may kill you (deduct 6 points from your STAMINA). If you do not have a lantern (oil alone is no good), you will surely die. If you survive the desperate remedy, turn to **40**.

5

Successive bursts of sheet lightning enable you to see that, all across the marsh, creatures resembling pumpkin-headed scarecrows are stirring. They are the Haggwort, formed of the earth and roused by the growing corruption in the land. Groaning, the mindless hulks rise and make their sluggish way towards Hustings, their paws gripping a variety of murderous weapons. They are great fighters, but they suffer one weakness: they are animated by mystic fires which are held under pressure within their heads; any cut to the head, no matter how tiny, will free the energy, and the sudden release will cause the Haggwort's head to explode! Hustings must be warned of the imminent attack, but a Haggwort stands on the road, in your way. Will you:

Attack it? Turn to **36**
Head out on to the moors in a bid to sneak round it?
Turn to **108**
Put on a Chameleon Cloak – if you have one?
Turn to **260**

6

The mystic bolt shoots past your head and crashes into the woman, turning her into a warty, croaking frog! It seems that one of the very sorcerers she had been objecting to was watching over the proceedings and decided to end them. To your dismay, the onlookers fall about with laughter, while the frog hops away to begin a new life. Will you now go and listen to the old beggar (turn to **219**) or to the man in black (turn to **137**)?

7

You open a small vial of Metal Rot and empty its contents all over the square iron panel which houses the lock to your cage (cross the vial off your *Adventure Sheet*). The thick gurgling fluid does its work in seconds, and the lock dissolves into thin air. Not having heard a thing, the jailer is caught unawares when you sneak up behind him and knock him unconscious. You step over his mountainous body and slip out of the jail. Now you will have to leave Royal Lendle before you are caught again. Will you leave the city by the South Gate, which opens straight out on to the Main Trade Route (turn to **272**), or by the nearer East Gate (turn to **60**)?

8

The Shadow Warrior you face carries no weapon; it is a master of the martial arts, and its deadly, rotted hands move with blurring speed. Each Attack Round, the Warrior has two attacks. Treat this combat as if you are fighting two opponents with identical ratings at the same time.

First SHADOW WARRIOR   SKILL 9   STAMINA 9

If you defeat the Warrior, turn to 335.

9

You watch as the convoy of wagons disappears in the distance, before you follow in its wake. Progress is slow and you spend a restless night, knowing that if you had gone with the circus you would be in Shattuck by now. In the morning you wake (restore 3 STAMINA points) and continue on your journey.

10

Another day passes before you reach a large stone bridge on the northern outskirts of Shattuck. The Circus of Dreams stands near by, its evening show in full swing. The clown in charge of the circus steps out from behind a wagon; she bows to you — as four more performers step out from the shadows behind her. They are all Mandrakes and they are coming for you! To stand and fight would be sheer folly, and they will probably catch you if you stay on the road. Nevertheless, will you run along the road to Shattuck (turn to **91**) or take a most desperate gamble and dive off the bridge into the deep river, many feet below (turn to **104**)?

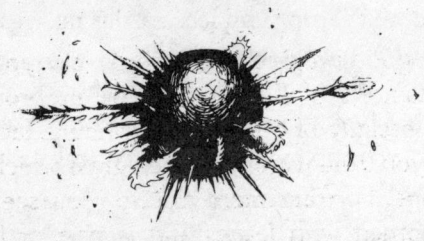

10

Sweat pours down your face and you fall backwards, tearing your mind free from this most hazardous device, an Orb of Mind-snaring. While it may not be the safest thing to carry around, perhaps it will have its uses. If you want to take it with you, add it to your *Adventure Sheet*. If you have not already done so, will you now study the sarcophagus (turn to **193**) or Hegmar's desk (turn to **147**), or do you ignore them both and leave (turn to **216**)?

11

You make good progress southwards, but you are still many miles north of Gornt when you are brought to a halt by the sight of a peculiar, grinning face that is watching you from within the deep grass which borders the roadside. Looking more closely, you see that the face is adorned with leaves and is part of the grass itself! It darts about, moving here and there as if blown by the wind; and it speaks in a spry and mischievous voice: ''Tis Jack-in-the-Green, the ancient king, here to offer you guidance. The world is dying, the soil corrupt and the trees astir with violence. Warriors five seek their lord, the one who must not be freed. Earth-mother seeks a healing hand, but 'tis proof of your worth she needs.' If you have a Green Leaf Brooch, turn to **398**. Otherwise, Jack-in-the-Green will offer you a chance to prove your worth. If you will accept his task, turn to **382**. If you do not, turn to **398**.

12

There's no time to rest. Night turns into day as you leave Hustings far behind and get your first view of the Witchtooth Line: a sprawling mass of unscalable mountain peaks, monster-filled caves and treacherous narrow passes. Adventurers who can say that they've 'crossed the Line' are the most respected of their kind. Eventually, you come to a bridge and, later, to a fork in the road. Will you go to the left (turn to **393**) or to the right (turn to **334**)?

13

Write down how many Gold Pieces you wish to gamble, then roll one die. On a roll of 2–6, turn to **54**; if you roll a 1, turn to **175**.

14

Because of the poor conditions, you spend much of your time concentrating on not falling over. The Crombane, however, have no such fears. Their howls rise and fall on the wind, and their revolting feet drum the earth behind you. If you have a set of Calthrops, you may throw them down in the Crombanes' path. The spiked metal balls will rip into their foul flesh and give you the time you so desperately need. If you wish to do this, cross the Calthrops off your *Adventure Sheet* and either make for the copse (turn to **63**), or run back northwestwards, to the road (turn to **160**). If you do not have – or do not wish to use – any Calthrops, you must fight (turn to **290**).

15

The old man calmly lifts a finger and points at a wall. In response, there is a loud click, and a secret panel slides open. 'That way lies freedom, but back south lies knowledge, while north lies the greatest reward *and* the greatest danger. It is ever my duty to set the tasks.' Who is this man and why does he keep on about tasks? Surely it can't be . . . no! You look back at the old man, but he has gone. Where will you go now: through the secret door (turn to **278**), or back out into the hall and then through the south door (turn to **68**), the north door (turn to **374**) or the west door (turn to **56**)?

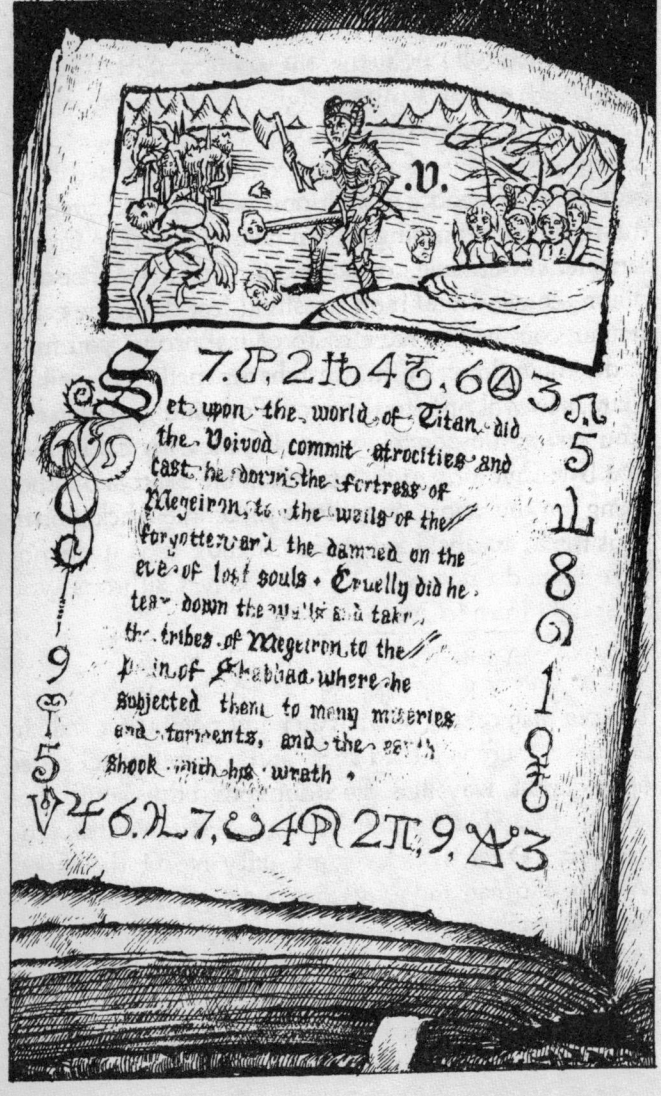

Set upon the world of Titan did the Voivod commit atrocities and cast he down the fortress of Megeiron, to the wails of the forgotten and the damned on the eve of lost souls. Cruelly did he tear down the walls and take the tribes of Megeiron to the Pit of Shabbad, where he subjected them to many miseries and torments, and the earth shook with his wrath.

16

In your hands is a page from the *Astrakkaans Numeris*, as laid down by Parcleasus, the numerologist. Though born blind, he has a mystic sight which has given him the gift of prophecy and the ability to chart the complex, unexplored realm of numbers. He has combined both gifts in the creation of this rare book, which predicts the return of Voivod and provides the numerological knowledge required to defeat him. Filled with horror, you read tales of Voivod's first existence on Titan; but you are relieved to see that the numerology is easy to understand. Basically, the system instructs you on how to turn words into numbers of mystical significance. You can turn any word into its numerological equivalent by converting each individual letter into a number, using the key below, and then by adding all the numbers thus found to create a mystical total.

1	2	3	4	5	6	7	8	9
A	B	C	D	E	F	G	H	I
J	K	L	M	N	O	P	Q	R
S	T	U	V	W	X	Y	Z	

For example, Royal Lendle is converted thus:

```
R O Y A L   L E N D L E
9 6 7 1 3   3 5 5 4 3 5
```

Add up all the numbers thus obtained, and you get 51. So 51 is the mystical number of Royal Lendle. As you will see later, this knowledge is vital to the completion of your quest.

17

There's no time to waste. You race forward and kick or push or grab and hurl any of the circus people who come within your reach to do whatever you can to send their bodies falling on to the campfire. Roll one die and add 2. The total rolled equals the number of Mandrakes you manage to destroy out of the original nine. Next, if you have any skins of oil, you may light them and throw them at the remaining Mandrakes; for each skin of oil you cross off your *Adventure Sheet*, you may destroy two Mandrakes. Any Mandrakes you destroy come from the bottom of the list, below. You must fight all the remaining ones at the same time. Though Mandrakes are not killed by normal combat, any you beat will be stunned for a few precious moments, allowing you to throw their bodies on to the fire.

	SKILL	STAMINA
CLOWN	9	10
First MANDRAKE	7	7
Second MANDRAKE	5	6
Third MANDRAKE	7	8
Fourth MANDRAKE	8	5
Fifth MANDRAKE	6	3
Sixth MANDRAKE	9	5
Seventh MANDRAKE	7	6
Eighth MANDRAKE	7	7

If you win, turn to **197**.

18

Thanking Osmani, God of Mercenaries, for your escape, you scramble up the ladder, push open the manhole cover with your hard head (deduct 1 point from your STAMINA) and haul yourself up into the open air. You roll over and shove the lid back in place. Restore 1 LUCK point for making a successful escape.

Resting briefly, you look around and see that you are in a short alley which leads into a busy square. And you are not alone. An impoverished jester has been watching your behaviour with a perplexed expression on her face. Her red-and-green outfit is in tatters, yet she manages a glib smile and walks towards you as you climb to your feet. 'Have you heard the one about the pig in a frenzy ...' she begins. You place the palm of your hand over her face and push her out of your way on to the floor. You're in no mood for jokes! Turn to **225**.

19

'Troubled times are ahead,' continues the enigmatic figure. 'To help you, the Horned God sends a gesture of goodwill: find the man of numbers, or his book. Without either, you will fail.' Then the face is gone. It seems that Jack-in-the-Green is a messenger for powerful elemental forces, forces which you decide to join. You will strive to be the Earth-mother's champion, against the evil of the Shadow Warriors.

Squinting through the blinding rain, you can just make out the lights and rooftops of Hustings. To the right of the town is a slender column of earth which has been forced up out of the ground by magic. Atop this hundred-foot-high pinnacle is a tower made of oozing, living sludge. You hear a slushing sound coming from somewhere just off the road and just as you look a flash of lightning reveals a man rising up out of the bog – at least it looks like a man. If you want to walk the few yards over to the figure, turn to **390**. If you would rather stay on the road, turn to **5**.

20

Two guards face you, but more are coming. You don't want to kill the men – after all, they are only doing their job – so you will have to use all your skill in a bid to disarm them. Without their swords, they will soon surrender and let you go. You must fight both of them at the same time, but if you win a round against the one you choose to fight, you do not injure him (because of this, the guards are not given STAMINA scores). But if your score in any Attack Round is 3 or more points higher than your opponent's, you have disarmed him and he no longer takes any part in the battle. Of course, the guards are trying to kill you and will cause damage to your STAMINA in the usual way if they wound you in any Attack Round.

	SKILL
First CITY GUARD	7
Second CITY GUARD	6

If you disarm both guards in six rounds of combat or less, you may leave the alleyway and flee into the temple grounds you saw earlier (turn to **164**); but if you do not manage to disarm them within this time, more guards appear and you are captured (turn to **199**).

21

Though you turn on your heel with lightning speed, you still catch the merest glimpse of the Gorgon's hideous face: the hag's skin is lined with evil and is framed by a writhing mass of vipers. A cry escapes your lips as you fall back and spin dizzily away. She steps after you, eager for your fall, but you stumble on, never looking back. You go on and on, until at last you are out of the caves altogether.

A stagnant pond lies just outside; you peer into it and are shocked by the sight of your reflection — your hair has turned grey, and your skin is stretched taut over your bones! And it is only now that you feel a slight stiffening in your muscles. Deduct 4 points from your STAMINA and, if you are still alive, turn to **80**.

22

Further up the street you come across a tattoo shop. A tasteless sign over the entrance reads: 'Roggmondo's — No Design Too Difficult, No Bit Of Skin Too Small'. Will you enter Roggmondo's (turn to **33**) or continue up the street, which seems to open out into some sort of crowded area (turn to **118**)?

23

Leaving the lady, you carry on searching through the dark streets of the town, starting with a hovel on your right. You walk in through the open doorway and wait for your eyes to adjust to the darkness. *Test your Luck*. If you are Lucky, turn to **226**. If you are Unlucky, turn to **53**.

24

Against all the odds, you have made it to the far path. Seeing your miraculous leap, the Warriors howl in frustration. They themselves cannot make the jump, since the far path offers too narrow a landing area for their horses. You fear that the riders will now split up and wait for you at both ends of the pass, but no. They screech and all race southwards. You sense that time is against them; perhaps they fear the oncoming dawn. Whatever the reason, you breathe a long, long sigh of relief. Turn to **102**.

25

The town of Hustings has been devastated by the Haggwort assault, and though you feel that you have done your best to help, your best may not have been good enough. Following the downcast Hustings refugees, you make your way along the south-bound road. If you have a Green Leaf Brooch, or if you have an iron band and the word 'Cerunnos' means something to you, turn to **397**. Otherwise, turn to **12**.

26

After unleashing a stream of abuse which has no effect, you finally shout, 'Your father is the son of a luteplayer and your mother has a face like a bucket of frogspawn.' At this, the jailer leaps to his feet and, despite his bulk, rushes swiftly towards you. Foam dribbles from his mouth as he unlocks the cage and lumbers in, fists at the ready. He won't accept any apologies.

JAILER   SKILL 8   STAMINA 7

If you win, you will have to leave the city before the alarm is raised. Will you leave by the South Gate, which opens out on to the Main Trade Route (turn to **272**), or by the nearer East Gate (turn to **60**)?

27

The town square is a cobbled area with, in its centre, an old cross. It is a hive of activity as wool-spinners, farmers, masons, artisans, merchants, drunkards, travellers, simple peasants and a whole variety of other folk go about, minding one another's business. After drawing a few blanks, you meet a local priestess who knows who you are speaking of. 'Ah,' she murmurs wisely, 'you mean Parcleasus, the numerologist who once lived here. Sadly, you are wasting your time. He went to the Forbidden Caves, home of the dreaded Gorgon, three years ago and, alas, never returned. He must have been turned to stone.' Though this news is all bad, you thank the priestess and walk away. But you have gone only a couple of steps when a beggar tugs at your sleeve and asks you for a Gold Piece. If you are willing to pay the beggar, cross off the Gold Piece from your *Adventure Sheet* and turn to **101**. If you can't or won't pay the beggar, turn to **159**.

28

Realizing that you are no match for the might of all five Warriors combined, you run back to the north. Your lungs burn as you try to put some distance between yourself and the shrieking phantoms. Fortunately, you come at last to a narrowing of the path which forces the Warriors to ride in single file. But one of them has sped ahead of the others in a bid to delay you. You must fight and destroy it before the rest catch up. Roll one die to see which of the five you must face. If you roll a 6, ignore the result and roll again. When you are told to continue your adventure, after defeating the Warrior, turn to **72** (note this on your *Adventure Sheet*). Now, if you roll:

1	Turn to 8
2	Turn to 394
3	Turn to 259
4	Turn to 183
5	Turn to 245
6	Roll again

29

You feel lightheaded and are just on the verge of agreeing to help with the dig — when you come to your senses, get a grip on yourself and politely refuse. However, rather than express any regrets or concern at your dizzy spell, Guignol raises his pick-axe and rushes, screaming, towards you. There is no reasoning with this man possessed.

GUIGNOL   SKILL 7   STAMINA 12

If you win, roll four dice and add the numbers together.

If the total is equal to or less than your current STAMINA score, turn to **62**. If the total is higher than your current STAMINA score, turn to **385**.

30

Leaving the tavern behind, you walk towards the sprawling market area in the centre of the city. Ironically, the market stands next to Royal Lendle's poorest district, a warren of dilapidated buildings housing beggars and thieves. All in all, it is a sad and dangerous place.

The sort of things you want would normally cost you a small fortune; luckily, you have a good many merchant friends, who will sell you their wares for next to nothing. The eastern side of the market is where you will find all the hardware you may need: weapons, basic equipment and so on. On the western side, more unusual items are to be found. Which side will you visit first, the eastern (turn to **82**) or the western (turn to **66**)?

31

A number of incredibly strong hands grab you from behind and pull you down on to the ground. Lying flat on your back, you look up to see Ennian, the Burgomeister of Gornt, standing over you. He smiles and says, 'Don't worry, you won't feel a thing. You'll soon be one of us.' Then he bends down and puts out his hand. It turns into a slimy, organic suction pad; he clamps it over your face and sends you into a sleep from which you never awaken.

32

Pushing yourself to the limit, you almost miss the low wire that is stretched across the passageway. You will have to jump, to avoid tripping over it. *Test your Skill*. If you succeed, turn to **278**. If you fail, turn to **297**.

33

Casting a swift glance over your shoulder, you turn the ornately carved door-knob of the tattoo parlour and enter. A tiny bell clinks overhead, shaking a drab little man out of his daydream. It is Roggmondo. He looks at you with a bored expression and asks, 'Tattoo, friend?' Do you reply 'Yes' (turn to **143**), or 'No' (turn to **270**)?

34

Hearing the gentle footsteps and the swishing of her gown, you try to avert your gaze — but too late! You look into the face of the Gorgon and must pay the ultimate price. Now there are seven statues in the cave again!

35

Running this way and that, you try to evade the hunting Orcs, but there are too many of them, and they soon have you trapped in a narrow gully. Even by Orc standards, this is a particularly mangy and ferocious bunch. Some train their bows and spears on you as their leader steps forward and grunts, 'We're the Orcs of the Black Scorpion, the toughest tribe in all the Witchteef. Surrender or die!' The tribal shaman, a gross hag, whispers words of counsel in her leader's ear; judging by her expression, her advice is evil in intent. If you agree to surrender, turn to **288**. If you would rather fight, turn to **377**.

36

Getting in a strike at the Haggwort's head will not be the easiest of things to do.

HAGGWORT   SKILL 11   STAMINA 2

If you win, you may go either to the town (turn to **367**), to the tower on the pinnacle (turn to **142**), or on to the treacherous moorlands (turn to **69**).

37

Caught in the open, you cannot hope to outrun the Warriors' horses or prevent yourself being cut down by the Warriors' vicious attack. Your adventure is over.

38

You opt for the oldest trick in the book. Groaning aloud, you clutch your side and fall to your knees in an act of epic agony. The jailer glances over his shoulder to see what all the fuss is about. *Test your Luck*. If you are Lucky, turn to **74**; if you are Unlucky, turn to **123**.

39

After a day of hard but swift travel, the circus stops on the north side of a huge stone bridge, on the outskirts of Shattuck. The menacing range of mountains known as the Witchtooth Line is clearly in sight, running before you like the teeth of a loathsome Earth-dragon. You stretch your stiff legs as the troupe unload the wagons and start to put up the tents and stalls; they intend to perform this very evening. When all is finished, three of the performers ride on into Shattuck to drum up custom. The remaining nine gather in a circle round a campfire. There, they eat and discuss the coming performance. For some reason, you are excluded from both the meal and the discussion. You walk about the encampment in a nervous and restless mood. You have a number of vague suspicions and feel that you must do something about these circus folk before the people from Shattuck arrive. If the name 'Korin' means anything to you, turn to **51**. If it does not, turn to **255**.

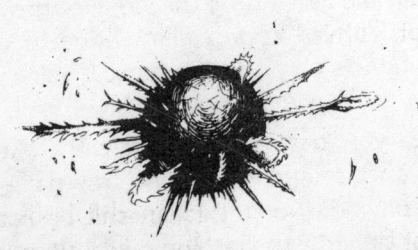

40

The Man-Orc fought with great ferocity, but you have defeated him. Such creatures usually dwell in isolated areas so, for him to be here in the city, your assailant must have been driven either by the promise of great rewards or by fear of a terrible punishment. Searching the swiftly decaying carcass, you find a small Black Key, which you may take if you want to (don't forget to add it to your *Adventure Sheet* if you do take it).

Soon you are walking through the South Gate, out of Royal Lendle and away from the scene of the assassination attempt. Turn to **145**.

41

Well done, you have chosen correctly. An ancient battle was once fought here, hence the name, and the thousands of bodies of the fallen still lie beneath the earth. What better place for Voivod to raise an army of the dead? You race to the Battle Plains and see him – the Voivod himself – an incredible force of timeless decay, ringed by his five lieutenants, the Shadow Warriors, who dance in darkest ecstasy. Beside the Voivod is an Iron Bell of Summoning. If Voivod strikes this magic artefact, the dead will rise to do his bidding. He must be stopped, but how? Just looking at Voivod is a shattering experience. If you arrived here *early*, turn to **189**. Otherwise, turn to **364**.

42

Seeing how well you handle yourself in a fight, the chief of the Big Boulder Orcs sends his mean-looking champion over to clobber you.

ORC CHAMPION   SKILL 8   STAMINA 7

If you win, you realize that if the Orcs of the Big Boulder are victorious they will kill you; and if the Orcs of the Black Scorpion triumph, Uggamonggo will expect you to stay with his tribe for years. So you flee. *Test your Luck*. If you are Lucky, turn to **350**. If you are Unlucky, turn to **119**.

43

'Tut tut tut! Not your day, is it?' Bartolph smirks condescendingly as he reaches out for your stake. Will you let him take the gold (turn to **151**) or grab his wrist and call him a cheat (turn to **140**)?

44

Your search for the hermit has used up a good deal of precious time. Unless you can find some way to make it up, you may very well reach Karnstein too late to save it. Eventually you rejoin the Weirtown road. If you wish to follow it back west, turn to **160**. If you would rather cut across country and head directly southwards (remembering that roads usually offer greater safety for the traveller), turn to **247**.

45

If you have read either Hegmar's Warning or the Circus Journal, turn to **17**. If you have read neither, turn to **315**.

46

It does not take long for the eager foot-soldier to reach you. Much as you dislike doing it, you will have to kill him before reinforcements arrive.

CITY GUARD   SKILL 8   STAMINA 8

If you defeat the guard in five or fewer rounds, you escape and may either rush out of the alley and up the street (turn to **360**), or down into the sewers (turn to **375**). If the guard is still alive after five rounds, you are captured by reinforcements and taken to the jail (turn to **199**).

47

It is with a growing sense of urgency that you cross the fields of heather and the windswept landscape which lies between Narbury and Shattuck. After a while you come to a rough-and-ready shelter: a ramshackle wooden door built across a rocky alcove. If you wish to investigate this shelter, turn to **178**. If you would

rather carry on towards the Main Trade Route, turn to **399**.

48

Your path takes you higher and higher into the mountains, where it's not only the Shadow Warriors you'll have to be wary of but all the other unwholesome denizens of the region. But for now, you have only the plaintive crying of the mountain winds to keep you company. After a while, your path descends to ground level, petering out near a large cavemouth which reeks of grim foreboding. Dare you enter the Forbidden Caves? If so, turn to **395**. If you would rather be on your way to Karnstein, turn to **80**.

49

Looking up, you see that the drapes have been lifted, to reveal a vampire-like creature rising from her throne. Her ghastly countenance is haggard with age. At her side is a living 'fireplace' which looks like the head of a Haggwort, only larger and more malevolent. It watches both you and the creature as she walks towards you and says, 'I am Urtha. Many years ago, when I was but a vampire, the peasants of this region destroyed me with the same wooden stake that now lies on that table. Though destroyed as an Undead, I was, like the ancient Haggwort, expelled from the grave. Now I am *beyond* undeath. I am a Wamphyr!

'Times are changing, the old regimes are being swept away. We are entering a twilight existence of which I shall be queen! And with this . . .' she lifts her wrist to display an iron band '... I can command the mindless Haggwort. Guided by my experience of centuries, they will make an unstoppable army!'

It is time to act. If you have a vial of Metal Rot, you may throw it at her iron band (turn to **83**). If you do not, will you attack her (turn to **305**) or ask her to prove her power (turn to **251**)?

50

Too late! Smegg is the veteran of a thousand betrayals; his spider-jaw blade cuts deep into your shoulder (deduct 2 points from your STAMINA). You must fight the wretch.

| SMEGG | SKILL 8 | STAMINA 3 |

If you win, turn to **71**.

51

The clues all add up: Korin said that 'they', who had been the cause of the troubles in Gornt, had left the very day you arrived, having been in Gornt for the previous seven days. According to the hand-out you found, the circus had been there for the same period and length of time. Following your hunch, you sneak close to the campfire and then pull the mirror out of your pack. Though half-prepared, you still have to stifle a cry of surprise when you see that each and every one of the circus performers is a disgusting Mandrake! You must protect the people of Shattuck from this spreading contagion of evil. If you have read Hegmar's Warning, turn to **17**. If you haven't, turn to **255**.

52

You take a deep breath and then start running towards the gate. *Test your Skill*. If you succeed, you make the jump and head towards the East Gate (turn to 301). If you fail, deduct 1 point from your STAMINA for bouncing off the hard gate; it is too high for you. You will now have to face any guards who have come after you along the narrow passage (turn to 20).

53

Before you know it, you are enveloped in a cloying mist which sends you into a deep sleep; turn to 186.

54

Your smile turns into a look of mute disbelief as the die suddenly flips over: your roll has become a 1. 'Too bad,' says Bartolph, reaching for your gold. The die he gave you is obviously loaded, and he is a trickster! If you want to grab his wrist and accuse him of cheating, turn to 115. However, if you would rather avoid any trouble and let him have the money, deduct the Gold Pieces you have lost from your *Adventure Sheet* and leave the tavern; turn to 30.

55

As soon as he sees you, the guard raises the alarm. You had better get this fight over and done with quickly.

MANDRAKE   SKILL 8   STAMINA 7

If you win in four rounds or fewer, you escape; turn to 300. If, however, the Mandrake is still alive after the end of the fourth round, turn to 31.

56

The door opens into a small storage room. Among the earthenware and bric-a-brac, you find two meals of Provisions, which you may take. Restore 1 LUCK point for this chance find. Now you will have to go back into the hall and choose another route. Will you go north (turn to **374**), south (turn to **68**), or east (turn to **89**)?

57

The crowd's reaction to your gamble is good – in fact it is too good, and you find yourself in the middle of a greed-crazed crush. City guards race forward to break up the stampede, a stampede which threatens to squash you. If you like, you can call out to the guards for help and give yourself up (turn to **199**). Otherwise, you will have to take your chances among a heap of clawing and grasping bodies. If you choose the latter course, roll one die and deduct from your STAMINA that many points.

If you survive, you may sneak out through one of the square's now unguarded exits. Will you escape over the green and pleasant grounds of a small temple, bordered by a low wall (turn to **164**), or run down a narrow lane (turn to **118**)?

58

Cupping your hands, you scoop the water up to your lips. The magical liquid makes your head spin as it takes immediate effect. Roll one die and follow the instructions in the table below.

Roll	Effects
1	Nothing happens
2	Restore 2 STAMINA points
3	Restore 1 LUCK and 2 STAMINA points
4	Restore 1 LUCK and 4 STAMINA points
5	Restore 2 LUCK and 4 STAMINA points
6	Restore 1 SKILL, 2 LUCK and 4 STAMINA points

You may drink from the well only once before moving on, either northwards (turn to 349) or back to the south (turn to 44).

59

You open the safe and find 10 Gold Pieces, which you may take (add them to your hoard on your *Adventure Sheet*). You are about to go over to examine the book when you hear a noise outside. You decide you had better leave the wagon before you are discovered. Return to 255 and choose an option you have not picked before.

60

Mere streets away from the huge East Gate, you come upon a rarity on the streets of Royal Lendle: a rubbish

61

cart standing unattended. A few citizens are wealthy and cultured enough not to throw their litter out of the window; instead, they save it for the Lendle rubbish collectors, who take it to a large quarry just beyond the city wall. Gate Wardens always stand watch over the four city gates as a matter of course, but now they could also be on the lookout for you. Therefore, you reckon it may be a good idea to sneak aboard the rubbish cart and hide among all the garbage. That way, you might just be able to slip through the gate unseen. If you decide to climb aboard the cart, turn to **126**; but if you would rather approach the East Gate in a more noble manner, on foot, turn to **301**.

61

Reluctantly you put some of the junk into your mouth – and immediately spit it out. It's alive! In fact, it's a

Slod-Kedbolm, whose skin is toxic. The sloppy black thing emits a high-pitched whine then slithers away. Its taste still has you heaving (deduct 2 points from your STAMINA). 'Is our food not to your liking, then?' a voice enquires. Turn to **49**.

62

Ashamed by what has happened, you wipe Guignol's blood off your hands. Why did he attack you? After all, he didn't seem to be evil! You feel sure that your unnatural dizziness was a part of what's going on here. Maybe you can find some clue in the campsite. Will you:

Search the site	Turn to **271**
Try to destroy the skeleton?	Turn to **294**
Leave the camp at once and continue your journey?	Turn to **282**

63

The weirdness shows no sign of abating as you enter the copse; nor do the twisted trees offer you any protection from the rain. Suddenly, a fork of lightning cuts down through the darkness and blasts a tree right in front of you. You take another path . . . but find your way blocked by another fork of lightning, and another and another! You run, but no matter which way you turn, you come close to being incinerated. It is only after several minutes of this deadly cat-and-mouse game that you realize you are being herded into the heart of the copse; there, you are confronted by a Mahogadon, a long-dormant tree monster that has been stirred into wakefulness by the changes in the earth. One of its boughs swoops down and lifts you up, its leafless branches wrapping round your waist. You cry out as the woody tentacle begins to squeeze the life out of you. If you have a vial of Sleeping Draught, turn to **200**. If you do not, you will have to fight; turn to **357**.

64

You leap aside just in time as the door swings wide open and slams into the wall with a loud bang. Dusting yourself down, you step inside the dark shelter. The place smells of Orc and is bare, save for some black robes and a torn map of Royal Lendle. Hidden under one of the robes is a metal casket. You try to open it, but it is locked. Do you have a Black Key or a vial of Metal Rot? If so, you may use either to open the casket (turn to **354** – and cross off Metal Rot from your *Adventure Sheet* if you use that); otherwise, or if you would rather leave the casket alone, turn to **248**.

65

Preparing a cauldron of cockroach and rat-droppings stew is a revolting, tedious and unappreciated chore – and Bonesquagg Grogmaker, the Orc chef, is only too quick to belabour you, should you make even the slightest mistake in preparation. Even worse punishment comes when you are forced to eat a bowl! The stuff makes you feel sick in the stomach, but it is still a crude form of nourishment (restore 2 points of STAMINA). Just as you are finishing your stew, the tribe's shaman has four Orcs seize you and manacle you to a blood-stained stretch rack! Then the sly, sniggering shaman defers respectfully to Uggamonggo, who says, 'My shaman reckonz yer on a secret mishun ta try an' find out our war planz. Now yoo'd better tell uzz what yer up to, or yoo'll gain a few inches.' Will you talk (turn to **198**) or keep quiet (turn to **269**)?

66

It does not take you long to find most of the things which may be of use to you during your adventure. Look at the list opposite and, if you buy any of the items described there, add it to your *Adventure Sheet*, deducting the appropriate number of Gold Pieces. Except for Provisions and the Amulet of Luck (which may be used at any time except during a battle) and the Ring of Agility (which may be used whenever you *Test Your Skill*), you may use items only when instructed to do so by the text. Finally, unless the list tells you otherwise, you may buy only one of each item.

Amulet of Luck	You may use this talisman once only, after which it is useless. Using it restores your LUCK score to its *Initial* level. Cost: 4 Gold Pieces
Chameleon Cloak	Woven by Elven craftsmen, this fine cape takes on the hue of any natural background. It is not so effective against man-made backgrounds such as brick walls, and it works best in the hours of darkness. Cost: 3 Gold Pieces
Fire-crackers	Thrown at a hard surface, these tiny magical devices explode with a loud noise and a blinding flash of light. Though harmless, they can frighten or shock opponents. You may buy any number of them. Cost: 2 Gold Pieces each
Mirror	Although seemingly useless, in the past mirrors have proved useful time and again in the course of your many adventures. Cost: 1 Gold Piece
Provisions	You may buy any number of meals. Cost: 1 Gold Piece per meal
Ring of Agility	Whenever you are told to *Test your Skill*, you may draw on the power of this magic ring. If you do so, deduct 2 from the die-roll. You must decide whether or not to use the ring before you make the roll; if you choose to use it, one use of the ring is spent, whether you succeed in the test or not. The ring may be used three times only, after which it is useless. Cost: 4 Gold Pieces
Sleeping Draught	One vial of this potent brew will knock even a Manticore out for days. You may buy any number of vials. Cost: 3 Gold Pieces each

If you have not yet visited the eastern side of the market, turn to **188**; if you have, turn to **321**.

67

One by one, the balls fall to the ground. Then you get a stinging kick on your backside and fall flat on your face. The circus folk roar with laughter as you pull off the ridiculous horse's head. The clown stands over you with a dry look and shakes her head. 'You're clearly no performer. For 3 Gold Pieces, you can buy your way.' If you pay the clown, cross the gold off your *Adventure Sheet* and turn to **77**. If you can't or won't pay, turn to **9**.

68

You enter a room packed with books and wax-sealed tubes containing ancient scrolls. The two Dark Elves who passed you in the hallway earlier sit at a large table reading magnificent tomes. But as soon as you enter, they look up and shout, 'Our temple has been profaned! Death to the outsider!' They draw long daggers from beneath their robes and lunge at you. You must fight them both at the same time.

	SKILL	STAMINA
First DARK ELF	7	5
Second DARK ELF	8	6

If you win, you may search the library (turn to **192**), or go back into the hall and enter the north door (turn to **374**), the east door (turn to **89**), or the west door (turn to **56**).

69

Shunning the safety of the road, you head deeper and deeper into the marsh. The Haggwort are all over the moors but they are too slow to bother you. However, the Haggwort are not the only source of danger on Hustings Moor. Almost too late, you see that you are about to tread on a rune-carved obsidian disc. It is some sort of mystic man-trap. *Test your Luck*. If you are Lucky, turn to **182**. If you are Unlucky, turn to **234**.

70

In the darkness of the sewers you cannot make out the Slygore's form at all clearly; all you know is that the creature is dark and malevolent. When you strike the Slygore, its 'skin' hisses and steams. It is acidic to the touch and it has dissolved your weapon (cross it off your *Adventure Sheet*). Worse still, a black maggoty slime has twitched its way up on to your hand, burning it. You howl and must deduct 2 points from your STAMINA. Then the Slygore gives vent to another unearthly moan and lifts its bulk, as if to come down on you and crush you. Will you flee (turn to **356**) or rummage swiftly through your pack for something which may defeat it (turn to **230**)?

71

Stepping over Smegg's repulsive little body, you return to the brightly lit chamber and the archway. Because the walls are emitting a faint glow, you decide to put out your lantern. Then you cross the room, pass through the arch and descend the long, wide staircase. The steps end at a corridor, which you follow until you come to a crossroads. Will you go north, back the way you came (turn to **106**), south (turn to **114**), east (turn to **122**) or west (turn to **144**)?

72

Made wary by your victory, the other Warriors rein their horses to a halt. As one, the four hiss with fear and hatred. But you don't stay to watch this display of evil: you run round a bend, putting yourself out of their sight. Then you hear the pounding of hoofs as the Warriors take up the pursuit once more. You won't be so lucky a second time: you need to find a way to shake them off. Will you attempt to hide in one of the many ruts in the rocky path (turn to **346**), hurriedly put on a Chameleon Cloak, if you have one, and hug the shadowy side of the looming rock-face (turn to **324**), or attempt a running jump across the deep ravine to the path on the other side of the pass (turn to **2**)?

73

All that stands between you and the Voivod are the Shadow Warriors. You must fight each of the Warriors (except any you have already banished by special means) one after the other. If you possess the Ring of Rabbam, remember to ignore the Warriors' special abilities. The paragraph for each Warrior is: **8, 394, 259, 183** and **245**. If you defeat all the Warriors, you may then face Voivod. If you do so carrying the Spear of Doom, turn to **171**. If you do so without the Spear, turn to **249**.

74

Concerned, the jailer walks over to your cage, unlocks it and rushes in to help you. You spring forward, snatch the keys from his pudgy hand and leap out of the cage.

You slam the door shut and lock it before the jailer has time to do a single thing. Then you throw away the key and leave the jail. The imprisoned man's cries echo behind you as you make your way out of the city. Will you leave by the South Gate, which opens out on to the Main Trade Route (turn to **272**), or by the nearer East Gate (turn to **60**)?

75

Putting the eerie ghost-town far behind you, you head roughly south-west until you come to a sheltered glade. There you lie down and catch a few hours' sleep (restore 2 STAMINA points).

When you wake up, it is to the dawn of a sunny day. Will you cut westwards and join the road to Shattuck (turn to **334**), or take the southbound road, which leads straight to the perilous Witchtooth Line (turn to **386**)?

76

Just when you think the hermit is about to go berserk, he falls to his knees, sobbing. Outside, the pleas grow more persistent, but Hammicus just presses his hands over his ears and weeps, 'Leave me in peace. You cannot be my son. My son is dead.' At this, the voice screams and fades into oblivion. The ordeal is over.

Rising, the hermit smiles through his tears and says, 'I owe you my life. In return I offer you knowledge. The Shadow Warriors are vessels of their master's will. They can be destroyed only when he is destroyed. But they *can* be banished. If you best a Warrior in combat, tear the facemask off its dissolving form. Separated

from its talisman, the Warrior will be doomed to limbo for a hundred years.'

If, in future, you defeat a Shadow Warrior, turn to **223** and *not* to **335** as instructed (make a note of this on your *Adventure Sheet*). Restore 1 LUCK point for obtaining this priceless information. Resting for the night, you leave the cottage next day at dawn and make your way back south. Turn to **44**.

77

The clown curtsies and declaims, 'Welcome to the Dream Circus; it brings fantasies to some and nightmares to others. You may ride with us to Shattuck.' You assume you are to ride inside the clown's wagon, but, when you go to open the door, her hand reaches out and grips your own. 'Don't!' she snaps. You turn angrily but are disarmed by her smile. 'I thought you would prefer to ride up front with me and my mute driver, Petulengro. Besides, my living-quarters are in such a mess.'

Keeping a tight rein on your suspicions, you follow the clown to the front of the wagon and take your seat as the wheels start to roll. The convoy makes excellent time. While you ride, will you ask the clown about the madness at Gornt (turn to **116**), about the Circus of Dreams (turn to **165**), about events at Karnstein (turn to **130**), or would you rather sit the ride out in silence (turn to **39**)?

78

With the guards in hot pursuit, you rush up the lane but pause when you notice a manhole in the middle of

the roadway. Suddenly it occurs to you: possibly you could lose the guards by sneaking down into the sewers. You are considering what to do when a fist-sized metal ball bounces in front of you then comes to a halt on the cobbles. It came from somewhere to your right. You look in that direction and see a mysterious figure, clad head to foot in black robes, scurrying away up a narrow alley between two buildings. Will you pick up the metal sphere (turn to **211**), leave it and go down into the sewers (turn to **375**), or ignore both options and keep on running up the street (turn to **22**)?

79

The book is a collection of 'Myths and Legends of the Old World'. On the off-chance, you look up Karnstein and discover two things of interest. First, it is said that

the area was once called Assur-Na-Menes, the site of a massive battle in which ten thousand men died. The task of burial was so great that the victors merely turned the soil of the battle plain over, covering the bodies where they lay. It is said that the bodies lie there still, beneath a layer of dry earth on which nothing grows. Another legend speaks of the Waster, a cruel tyrant whose very tread could despoil the earth. After seven days of this, the suffering soil arose and trapped the Waster, imprisoning him at a place now called the Zarrikiz Shrine.

You close the book, just as a secret panel slides open in the far wall. Do you have a Chameleon Cloak? If so, turn to **127**; if not, turn to **150**.

80

Putting the caves behind you, you follow the edge of the Witchtooth Line eastwards until you come to the Main Trade Route once more. You cross a bridge and take a mountain trail, which should bring you to Karnstein. You walk for quite some time and ... wait a minute! Where are you? Somehow you have left the road and now, in your daydreaming, you have come to a rocky clearing, in which stands a most spectacular sight. A man is standing here, sweating in the bright sun. He has been trying to dig a skeleton out of the rock-face – but what a skeleton! It is huge and belongs to a creature, the like of which you have never seen before. Seeing you, the man calls out, 'Ho, there! I am Guignol, an archaeologist from Chalannabrad, and I am on an excavation of vital academic import. I plan to take this unique specimen back to Femphrey. Unfortunately, I came on this venture alone, and now I find myself in need of aid. If you help me free the specimen, I'll pay you a hundred Gold Pieces.' While this sum is tempting beyond belief, you know that it will take hours to free the skeleton. If you accept the offer, turn to **385**. If, on the other hand, you would rather be on your way, turn to **210**.

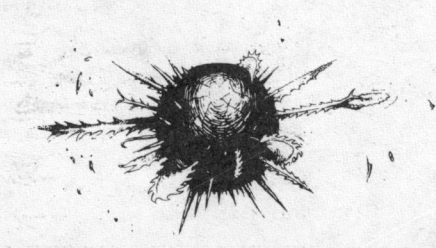

81

Do you have a vial of Sleeping Draught? If you have, turn to **244**; if you haven't, turn to **65**.

82

It does not take you long to find most of the articles which you hope will be of use to you during your adventure. Read through the list below and, if you buy any of the items described there, add it to your *Adventure Sheet*, remembering to deduct the stated number of Gold Pieces. Except for the battle-axe and the armour, you may use items only when you are instructed to do so by the text. Unless it is stated otherwise, you may buy only one of any article.

Battle-axe	Each time you hit your opponent in combat, you cause it to lose 4 STAMINA points (6 points if you *Test your Luck* and are Lucky; 2 if Unlucky). However, because of the axe's weight, you have to suffer a penalty: deduct 1 from your Attack Strength rolls whenever you use it. If you buy the battle-axe, enter it in the Weapon box of your *Adventure Sheet*. Cost: 3 Gold Pieces
Calthrops	These spiked metal balls are thrown to the ground in order to deter pursuit. You may buy any number of sets. Cost: 1 Gold Piece per set
Chainmail armour	Each time you are hit in combat, you lose only 1 STAMINA point (0 points if you *Test your Luck* and are Lucky; 2 if Unlucky). However, due to the armour's bulk, you must add 1 every time you are called upon to *Test your Skill*. The armour protects you only from damage gained in battles and is useless after it has taken 10 hits. Cost: 3 Gold Pieces

Lantern and oil	Useful in dark places. Cost: 1 Gold Piece for a lantern plus one skin of oil Each use of the lantern consumes one skin of oil. You may buy any number of additional skins (but not lanterns). Cost: 1 Gold Piece per skin
Manacles	These chains can bind most humanoid creatures. Cost: 2 Gold Pieces
Metal Rot	This alchemical solution dissolves most known metals but leaves flesh unharmed. You may buy any number of vials. Cost: 4 Gold Pieces per vial
Rope and grapple	About twenty metres of thin, lightweight rope, with a small metal hook affixed to one end. Cost: 4 Gold Pieces

If you have not already visited the western side of the market, turn to **188**; if you have, turn to **321**.

83

Shrugging off the strong grip of your guards, you grab a vial of Metal Rot and hurl it at the iron band. If your aim is good, the glass vial will break and spill its contents all over the band. Cross the vial off your *Adventure Sheet*, and then *Test your Skill*. If you succeed, turn to **331**. If you fail, turn to **305**.

84

When you rush out into the street at the far end of the alley, there is no sign of the woman. But you can hear footsteps coming up the alley behind you, so you keep on running. Wherever you go, you see more and more examples of chaos, all caused by the strange smiling people the woman called 'Mandrakes': they are powerful fighters who bleed green blood but never seem to die. Their opponents, the real inhabitants of Gornt, are totally outclassed. But the Mandrakes don't kill their human foes unless they have to; they prefer to render their victims unconscious so that they can drag them off, who knows where. You wish that there was something you could do to help the oppressed townsfolk, but the shouting and the footsteps dogging your heels remind you only too clearly that you yourself are still in peril. Now you can either keep heading the way you are going, towards the South Gate (turn to **184**), or you can veer off and head for the nearest portion of the town wall (turn to **207**).

85

The coil of veins crawls further up your arm, before suddenly falling away. You feel no ill-effects and are just wondering what all this has been about – when you see that the thing on the stone slab is changing shape; moreover, it is taking on *your* likeness!

The Mandrake replica rises from the slab and attacks you. If it kills you, it will take your place in society and no one will ever be the wiser. The Mandrake does not possess any armour or special equipment, but it does have the same weapon as you. It also has current SKILL and STAMINA scores identical to your own. Mandrakes are usually well-nigh indestructible, but if you defeat it now, while it is still newly formed, it will return to its pod-like shape.

If you win, you will have to *Test your Luck* to see whether the noise of your fight has alerted the others. If you are Lucky, return to **255** and choose an option you have not had before. If you are Unlucky, turn to **315**.

86

Rubbing his well-manicured hands in unrestrained glee, Bartolph sits beside you and hands you a die. 'Put some gold on the table as a stake,' he says, 'and roll the die. If you roll 4 or above, you win: you keep your stake-money and you take an amount equal to your stake from my own purse. If you roll less than 4 you lose, and I keep your stake. Easy, eh?' Yes, you think, almost too easy. A small crowd, drawn by the exaggerated loudness of Bartolph's voice, gathers round to watch. Decide how many Gold Pieces you wish to gamble and note the amount on your *Adventure Sheet*. Roll one die: on a roll of 4–6, turn to **54**; on 1–3, turn to **43**.

87

In the struggle, a torch is knocked over on to some highly inflammable chemicals, and soon the lab is ablaze. You make a hurried dash for the exit; on the way out, you may grab one of the following items which are lying about the place: a sword, a pack holding 2 Provisions, a ceramic mongoose paperweight, or a lantern and one skin of oil. Then you race down the staircase, turning a deaf ear to Kauderwelsch's screams. Only when you reach the road to the south of Cumbleside do you stop to look back. The entire tower is engulfed in flames. Then you look away, and continue southwest, into a sheltered glade where you sleep for a few hours (restore 2 points of STAMINA).

When you wake up, it is to the dawn of a sunny day. Will you cut westwards and join the road to Shattuck (turn to **334**), or take the southern road which leads straight to the Witchtooth Line (turn to **386**)?

88

You don't let anything distract you as you run over the slick, quaking ground. However, the way ahead is blocked by the huge mound. Will you approach the screaming face (turn to **378**), make for the copse which is off to your right, in the hope of veering back south later (turn to **63**), or retreat and head back north-west, towards the road (turn to **160**)?

89

You have entered the cultists' dormitory, a small room containing bunk beds and basic washing facilities. At first the place appears to be empty, but then an old man steps out from the shadows. Though clad in the robes of a cultist, he is human. He fixes you with a penetrating stare, his lined face displaying wisdom beyond years. 'I was wondering when you'd get here. You shun the tasks, yet take on a quest as dangerous as *this*!' He steps forward. Will you strike him (turn to **156**) or wait to see what he does next (turn to **15**)?

90

Once your dizziness clears, you find yourself standing at the foot of a grassy hill crowned by a circle of ancient standing stones. You have been transported to Cauldon Ring, heartland of the elemental gods. An awe-inspiring vision of the Horned God fills the skies, while the ghostly Sisters of Time dance within the circle. They are the past, present and future manifestations of the Earth-mother, and they guard the Spear of Doom. The Horned God speaks to you with a voice like the crashing of waves: 'You have been chosen to face Voivod, Lord of the Shadow Warriors. We once made the error of trying to burn out his fire, but could only imprison him. In the millennia which have passed, we have made good our error and have forged the Spear of Doom, which gives death to the living, and life to the dead. Take it, and use it wisely.'

All at once you discover the Spear in your hands, and you start to feel dizzy once more. Enter the Spear in the Equipment box of your *Adventure Sheet*, together with its Life-force, which you find by rolling one die and adding 5. The Spear is *not* a normal weapon: you may use it instead of normal combat (you must decide whether or not to do so *before* you start any fight) and it will automatically defeat your foe – but you must also deduct one point from the Spear's Life-force. If its Life-force drops to zero, the Spear becomes useless. Now, restore 6 points to your STAMINA and, if you came here from Hustings, turn to **12**; otherwise, turn to **399**.

91

Your bid for freedom ends in failure. The Mandrakes seize you and take you into one of the wagons, where a disgusting sight awaits. They press you up against a throbbing, man-sized vegetable pod. The thing starts changing shape. It is taking on your likeness! You die here, but other people will later insist that they have met you, only you've changed in some way. In fact, they'd swear that you no longer seem to be yourself!

92

You hear a loud snapping sound – the highwayman has fired his crossbow! Fortunately, his aim is none too steady. *Test your Luck*. If you are Lucky, the shot misses you; if you are Unlucky, however, the shot finds its mark and you must deduct 3 points from your STAMINA. If you survive the attack, you must fend off the highwayman, who has now drawn his shortsword.

HIGHWAYMAN   SKILL 7   STAMINA 6

If you win, turn to **274**.

93

You can think of many things you'd like to do in your lifetime, but scrubbing the filth off forty Orcish boots isn't one of them. Just as you finish scrubbing your last boot, the tribe's shaman orders four Orcs to seize you. She has them manacle you to a blood-stained stretch rack. Then she dutifully steps aside as Uggamonggo walks forward. He grunts, 'My shaman reckonz yer on a secret mishun ta try an' find out our war planz. Now yoo'd better tell uzz what yer up to, or yoo'll gain a few inches.' Will you talk (turn to **198**) or keep quiet (turn to **269**)?

94

Note on your *Adventure Sheet* how many Gold Pieces you wish to risk and then roll one die. On a roll of 3–6, turn to **54**; on a roll of 1 or 2, turn to **162**.

95

You stand dead still as Smegg waves grandly about him and says, 'We on the door of Elfie temple. No go. No safe. Me Smegg of the secret ways. Past the Elfies. Got rope for climb down safe hole. Smeggies route, it is. Can take you. Must take you. Must come or die. Elfies kill. Go any place by Smeggies route.' He walks over to you and shows you the long coils of stout rope he is carrying over his shoulder. 'Smeggies rope,' he says proudly. If you ask Smegg to take you south, turn to **224**. If you would rather make your way alone, turn to **50**.

96

After some time, you arrive once more at the bridge you crossed earlier, only now it is guarded. Silhouetted against the sky is the brooding, mounted form of a Shadow Warrior! It sees you almost at once and shouts out its terrifying cry. Roll one die to see which of the five Warriors you must fight. If you roll a 6, ignore the result and roll again. When, after defeating the Warrior, you are told to continue your adventure, turn to 11 (note this on your *Adventure Sheet*). If you roll:

1	Turn to 8
2	Turn to 394
3	Turn to 259
4	Turn to 183
5	Turn to 245
6	Roll again

97

You hurry across to the old armourer, who soon has you outfitted to your requirements: you may take a sword and a suit of Plate Armour. The Plate can take five hits before it becomes useless. If you are hit while wearing the Plate, you lose *no* STAMINA points. However, if you have to *Test your Skill* while wearing it, you must add 2 to your roll. Make a note of anything you wish to take in the appropriate boxes of your *Adventure Sheet* (remembering to cross off any weapons or armour you may already have). You are just about finished when you hear Wulf shout, 'Duck!' *Test your Luck*. If you are Lucky, turn to 323; if you are Unlucky, turn to 241.

98

The moment you touch the sphere, its sides flick open. Vicious blades, piercing spikes and slicing razors spring out in all directions. Roll one die to see how many of the projections injure you. For each wound, roll another die and deduct that many points from your STAMINA. If you are still alive, you may attack the Man-Orc (turn to **132**), try to expose him for what he really is (turn to **310**), or ignore him and go to the bar (turn to **3**).

99

The lady looks at you as you look dubiously at a boiled potato. 'Is something wrong?' she asks coyly. 'I wouldn't have thought someone with as marvellous a brain as yours would be so suspicious.' Will you apologize and eat the food she has kindly prepared for you (turn to **235**), ignore the food and try to engage her in conversation (turn to **173**), or leave the tower and go out to search through the menace-laden streets of Cumbleside (turn to **23**)?

100

You cross your fingers and step over the edge. *Test your Skill*. If you succeed, turn to **238**; if you fail, turn to **203**.

101

'Don't take no notice of 'er,' says the beggar, waving a dismissive hand at the priestess. 'She don't know nuffin' wiv all 'er books, she's ficker'n a frog in a fog. Da man o' numbers ain't stone. 'E couldn't 'ave seen no Gorgon, cause 'e's blind.' You don't even have time to thank the beggar for this valuable tip before he's heading in the direction of the nearest tavern, clutching his Gold Piece. Sadly you shake your head. Turn to **159**.

102

The 200 Gold Pieces you have been promised as payment is no longer important. Mendokan and his people were under your protection and you have failed them. The Shadow Warriors' power is awesome, unlike anything you have ever seen before; but you shall defeat these dark riders, you shall avenge all the innocent folk whom they have slain. For surviving the ambush, you may add 2 points to your LUCK.

It is dawn when you reach the southern exit of the Magyaar Pass, a place you will always remember as the scene of your greatest defeat. You stop to rest and consider your next move. The road to Karnstein leads straight to the south. Until you get there, more villagers will suffer or die each night. To the east, however, lives an all-knowing hermit; maybe you should learn all there is to know about these seemingly indestructible Warriors before you go rushing into battle. The hermit, alone, may possess such esoteric knowledge. Will you head south to Karnstein (turn to **11**) or east in search of the hermit (turn to **113**)?

103

As casually as you can, you reply, 'No, I'm needed elsewhere.' The clown glowers at you for an instant. Then she smiles, and the moment passes. Restore 1 LUCK point and turn to **39**.

104

Seizing your chance, you leap off the edge of the bridge and dive down, down, down, into the murky waters below. Though you have thwarted the Mandrakes, you have leapt out of the frying pan into the fire. You are barely able to stay afloat, as you find yourself caught in the famous Tass rapids. If you are wearing any armour, you will have to drag it off before it pulls you under (cross it off your *Adventure Sheet*). Your body is carried downstream at amazing speed. But as the river races through a mountain valley, you fear you will be smashed against the increasing number of boulders littering the middle of the river. *Test your Skill* six times, in order to avoid the rocks. Each time you fail a test, deduct 3 points from your STAMINA. If you survive this battering, you are washed up on the river's edge – on the south side of the Witchtooth Mountains! Dazed, bruised and exhausted, you fall asleep.

When you wake up, it is to a new day. You continue on your way, following the perimeter of the mountains, south-eastwards. In time you come to a large cavemouth. If you wish to enter the cave, turn to **395**; but if you would rather pass it by and continue eastwards, turn to **80**.

105

You soon arrive at the wood-and-glass door of 'Hegmar's Sanctum'. Within, all is dark and nothing stirs; the magician is nowhere to be seen. However, the door is open, so you slip inside and close it behind you. Hiding in the shadows, you watch as your pursuers rush right past. You wait for the sound of their steps to recede before coming out of cover. You are in Hegmar's showroom, a small place cluttered with objects of all kinds. It is strange that Hegmar should leave his expensive wares unattended, but you don't give this fact much thought as you study your surroundings. Only three things seem to be of any particular interest. Will you go over to the magician's desk (turn to **147**), hide in an ancient sarcophagus (turn to **193**) or study a smooth crystal sphere mounted on an ivory pedestal (turn to **312**); or do you prefer to leave them all alone and hurry out of the sanctum, to continue your flight from the guards (turn to **216**)?

106

Descending a long, wide staircase, you come to a crossroads. Will you go:

North?	Turn to **169**
South?	Turn to **114**
East?	Turn to **122**
West?	Turn to **144**

107

A handful of the Burgomeister's ghoulish servants are coming down the alley to his aid and are almost upon you. Desperate, you shove Ennian away and run off up the alley. But this action will achieve nothing unless you can exploit it. If you have a Fire-cracker, turn to **347**. Otherwise, turn to **31**.

108

Dodging the menacing form of the Haggwort, you strike out across the moors – only to fall into a sinkhole. Soon you are waist deep in quicksand ... and sinking fast. If you have a rope and grapple, you swiftly throw the hook round the branch of a tree and pull yourself out; turn to **168**. If you do not have a rope, you will have to climb out. *Test your Skill* twice. If you succeed in both tests, turn to **168**; but if you fail in either or both of them, turn to **117**.

109

Guignol cries, 'We've done it. The skeleton is now ready for transportation.' But you are not interested in any of this, as you have been suddenly overcome by a strange dizzy feeling. A red haze has descended over your vision, and when you next look at Guignol it is with uncontrollable hatred. Terror crosses his face as you dive, snarling, towards him.

GUIGNOL   SKILL 7   STAMINA 12

If you win, turn to **185**.

110

Some of the barrows can be flipped over with a nudge of the shoulder; other stalls are large affairs requiring a hefty shove. Whatever the method, the result is the same: chaos. The guards get caught up in a tangle of vegetables and angry traders, hurling abuse in their distinctive accent. Smiling, you grab some food (add two meals' worth of Provisions to your *Adventure Sheet*) and are about to head up the narrow street when you trip over a pile of spilt mangoes. *Test your Skill*. If you succeed, you may continue on your way (turn to **78**); but if you fail, you stumble and are captured by the guards (turn to **199**).

111

Most of the Shadow Warriors ride on, out of sight, but one of them wheels his horse round and thunders towards you! You run back into the darkest corner of the shelter and wait. Tense seconds pass in silence, and then the Shadow Warrior appears in the doorway, screeching its fury. Roll one die to see which of the five you must face. When, after defeating the Warrior, you are told to continue your adventure, you flee eastwards and must turn to **399** (note this on your *Adventure Sheet*). If you roll:

1	Turn to **8**
2	Turn to **394**
3	Turn to **259**
4	Turn to **183**
5	Turn to **245**
6	Roll again

112

You have the door open in no time at all, revealing a squalid cell. A ragged old man steps out and gasps, 'Free at last! You have the heartfelt thanks of Parcleasus the numerologist. Believing the Gorgon to be dead, I came to these Forbidden Caves on a quest for knowledge. Little did I think that she had been revived by an evil necromancer, who also set about filling her caves with such tricks as the illusory sound of snakes. She was unable to freeze me because my eyes are blind, I use mystic sight. But what of you?' Sensing Parcleasus's goodness, you tell him everything. When you have finished he says, 'This must be more than coincidence. You cannot hope to defeat Voivod without this.' He pulls a crumpled piece of paper out of his tunic and gives it to you. 'This is the most vital page of my Science of Numbers. Take it; it will reveal all.'

You can study the page now or at any time in the future by turning to **16** (make a note of this number on your *Adventure Sheet*). Your work here completed, you lead Parcleasus out of the cave. He clasps your hand in fellowship and bids you farewell. Then he makes for Shattuck, while you must go to Karnstein; turn to **80**.

113

You make straight towards the east and soon come to a large bridge. You cross it and join the Weirtown road, which you follow until you reach the region of low, wooded hills where the hermit is said to live — an area also renowned for its highwaymen! The sun is sinking when you leave the road and take a winding trail northwards, up on to the high ground. There, you find a famous landmark, the Wizard's Well. An old wizardly face, carved in a low overhang of moss-covered rock, looks down on a magic spring. Only good can come from partaking of this fluid. Will you pause to drink from the Wizard's Well (turn to **194**), or continue on your way (turn to **349**)?

114

Descending a long, wide staircase, you come to a crossroads. Will you go:

North?	Turn to **106**
South?	Turn to **187**
East?	Turn to **232**
West?	Turn to **144**

115

Test your Luck. If you are Lucky, turn to **222**; if you are Unlucky, turn to **140**.

116

'Gornt?' she asks lightly. 'Yes, we were there until yesterday when everything seemed to go insane. Indeed it was the barbaric, crazy behaviour of the townsfolk that led to our premature and hurried departure. We were frightened for our very lives. My magician, Monty Caphisto, reckons that it must have been something in the water.' You notice a hint of a smirk pass fleetingly over the clown's lips. 'But what about you?' she asks lightly. 'Would you care to join the Circus of Dreams permanently?' Will you answer yes (turn to **148**) or no (turn to **103**)?

117

Soon the only sign of your ever having been on the marsh is the rapid flow of air-bubbles that break the surface of the quicksand – before trailing to a halt.

118

The street opens out on to a round court, which is jammed solid with people; it is the famous Ranters' Corner. Here people stand on boxes and make speeches on any subject they like. In return, the crowds often heckle the 'ranters', as the speakers are called. You rush into the sea of bodies and momentarily shake off all pursuit. The guards find it hard to push through the crowds, who are not slow in voicing their resentment at being shoved about. In the event of any public unrest, some guards always occupy the corner; the marshal of these men is now making his way over to the guards following you, no doubt to demand an explanation. Despite your peril, you cannot resist hanging around and listening to the various ranters. Will you listen to an earnest young lady (turn to **289**), a ragged old man (turn to **219**), or a man in black who raves and shouts at his browbeaten audience (turn to **137**)?

119

Your excitement at having escaped from the tribe fades when you see dozens of small arrows fly over you. However, the arrows aren't coming from the Orcs of the Black Scorpion but are going towards them. Their rivals, the Orcs of the Big Boulder, are launching a surprise attack. One of the arrows hits you in the side (deduct 2 points from your STAMINA). Will you forgive this slight error in their aim and offer your services to the Orcs of the Big Boulder, hoping to avenge your earlier captivity (turn to **377**), or are you content to let the Orcs get on with their own fighting, and head southwards before you are seen (turn to **282**)?

120

You snatch the amulet from the Man-Orc's neck, drop it on the floor and crush it underfoot. The effect is instantaneous: the veterans realize the deceit played upon them at once, and their fury at being duped is beyond compare. Once they have finished with the Orc, the oldest of the veterans turns to face you. 'Accept my apologies,' he says, 'we were foolish. Maybe we have been living in the past for too long. Let us put all this behind us, and may a real peace between the nations start here, in this humble tavern.' In no time at all it is as if the four of you have always been the best of friends, and it is with some reluctance that you rise to continue on your journey.

When you step outside the door, however, you find yourself staring into the playful eyes of Jack-in-the-Green. 'Peace in Narbury is yours,' he says. 'Now a token and advice. Go straight to the ring which is too big for your finger.' Then he is gone. If you do not already have a Green Leaf Brooch, you find one in your pocket – add it to your *Adventure Sheet*. Now, will you head back east towards the Main Trade Route (turn to **267**), or cut across country so that you can rejoin the Trade Route much further south (turn to **47**)?

121

'There is too much corruption in the world,' says Jack-in-the-Green. 'The sleepers who should not be disturbed have been aroused. Your task is to lay Hustings to rest. Let the earth reclaim its own – but be warned! Violence can never be the final answer. Evil must be left to consume itself. Your duty is to help, not to beget further chaos. When you think you have succeeded, say the word "Cerunnos" in your mind and we will see what unfolds.' Make a note on your *Adventure Sheet* of this word, and turn to **19**.

122

Descending a long, wide staircase, you come to a crossroads. Will you go:

North?	Turn to **169**
South?	Turn to **114**
East?	Turn to **232**
West?	Turn to **253**

123

The jailer bellows with laughter at your terrible performance; he just cannot believe that you have tried to pull such an ancient stunt. Then he returns to his book, giggling now and then at your atrocious acting. You will have to try something else. Will you pour Metal Rot, if you have any, on to the lock of the cage (turn to **7**), hurl an insult at the jailer in the hope that he will come into your cell to punish you, giving you a chance to overpower him (turn to **26**), or abandon all hope and wait for the dungeon-wagon (turn to **208**)?

124

Though the walls of the pit are sheer, you use your rope and hook to climb up and make an easy escape.

125

You put the rope back in your pack and walk on. Soon you come to a junction. Will you go:

Left?	Turn to **296**
Right?	Turn to **217**
Straight on?	Turn to **139**
Back the way you came, and out of the caves?	Turn to **80**

125

You hurl the Fire-cracker to the floor (cross it off your *Adventure Sheet*). BANG!!! Both Kauderwelsch and her monster are stunned, giving you time to unbuckle the straps that are holding you down. If you have a weapon, you may hastily snatch it up before fighting the monster.

KAUDERWELSCH MONSTER

SKILL 8   STAMINA 14

If you win, turn to **87**.

126

It can hardly be said that you are travelling in luxury. The stench of the rubbish strewn over your body is truly revolting. Worse still, a contagious, turquoise mould has started to creep across your belongings. While it will not harm you, it does make your food unfit to eat. If you are carrying any Provisions, cross two meals off your *Adventure Sheet*. After much pitching and tossing, the vehicle reaches the East Gate. Turn to 301.

127

Two cultists step out of the secret passage. Before they can see you, you drop to the floor and throw the Chameleon Cloak over yourself. The Dark Elves sit down and talk. Behind them, the secret door starts to slide shut. Now, if you want to, you may hurry through the secret door before it shuts (turn to 295). Otherwise, you will have to go back out into the hall and choose either the north door (turn to 374), the east door (turn to 89) or the west door (turn to 56). Whichever way you go, you take off the Chameleon Cloak and return it to your pack once you have left the library. Because the Dark Elves remain inside the library, you dare not risk returning here again. Note on your *Adventure Sheet* that you may not choose 68 again.

128

Casually averting your gaze, you take the sphere from your pack and hand it over to the highwayman. His eyes open wide with pleasure – he cannot believe that he has earned such a prize. Yet as the crystal starts to glow, his smile fades into a gaze of dull stupor. The orb has stolen his mind! Carefully you return the sphere to your pack, then prod the body of the highwayman. Though still alive, he falls to the ground, mindless. You consider searching the body, but can't bring yourself to do it. Will you now drink at the Wizard's Well (turn to **58**), go north in search of the hermit, whom the highwayman claimed to have killed (turn to **349**), or leave the area altogether and head back south (turn to **44**)?

129

You shake off your unseen assailant's hand and spin around. Though you can't see the woman at all well, you can clearly hear her begging you to stay your hand. If you now do as she asks, turn to **158**; but if you reckon that it's just a trap, press on with your attack.

ASSAILANT   SKILL 6   STAMINA 8

If you win, turn to **31**.

130

'I know only that Karnstein is a boring little village in the middle of nowhere, and that it was once the site of some ancient battle. Why do you ask?'

Deliberately avoiding any details, you reply, 'I've heard rumours of trouble there, fighting with strange creatures. Someone will want a sword for hire.'

She murmurs thoughtfully, 'Strange creatures, eh? Good. We could do with some competition.' Then she snaps out of her daze and says, 'If it's money you want, forget Karnstein. Why don't you join our circus . . .

permanently?' The offer takes you by surprise. Do you answer yes (turn to **148**) or no (turn to **103**)?

131

Your fingertips barely scrape the edge of the far path, and it is with a lurching sense of horror that you realize you are falling into the deep crevice. The rocky ground rises to meet you. Your quest is over.

132

Stars and swirling fog cloud your vision as you lunge for the Man-Orc – the landlord has coshed you (deduct 2 points from your STAMINA).

When you wake up, miles back east on the road you came along, you see that the veterans have looted your body: cross off all your gold, your weapon and armour from your *Adventure Sheet*. It would be suicidal to go back to the Burning Balrog Inn, so you decide to continue towards Karnstein. If you wish to keep going to the east, back to the Main Trade Route, turn to **267**. If you would rather cut across country and rejoin the Main Trade Route much further south, turn to **47**.

133

Voivod strikes at you, and your body is cut into many pieces before it hits the ground again. The Earth-mother and the Horned God shall weep at your failure, for your failure means the end of all life.

134

Woad's shrieks ring in your ears as you spring up the broad street – only to see more guards ahead of you! Alerted by the shouts of your pursuers, these men draw their swords and attempt to block your route. The only way out of this trap is through a house standing to your right. Without a moment's hesitation, you open the door to this ramshackle place and enter. *Test your Luck*. If you are Lucky, turn to **277**; if you are Unlucky, turn to **166**.

135

All is dark and a storm rages overhead as you make your way towards Hustings. The road is little more than a track that winds its way across the infamous Hustings moors and, because of the downpour, is submerged in places, becoming part of the mire. Wary of encroaching quicksand, you press on, your efforts aided by the occasional lightning flashes of the storm. Suddenly you catch sight of a peculiar, grinning face. At first you think that someone must be hiding in the reeds, but then you realize that the leafy face *is* the reeds, moving from clump to clump as if blown by the wind. It speaks in a spry and mischievous voice: ''Tis Jack-in-the-Green, the ancient king, here to offer you guidance. The world is dying, the soil corrupt and the trees astir with violence. Warriors five seek their lord, the one who must not be freed. Earth-mother seeks a healing hand, but 'tis proof of your worth she needs.' If you have a Green Leaf Brooch, turn to **19**. Otherwise, Jack-in-the-Green will offer you a chance to prove your worth. If you will accept his task, turn to **121**. If not, turn to **19**.

136

'Yoo don't expect uzz ta believe that rubbish, do yoo?' sneers the shaman. Uggamonggo doesn't believe a word of it either. The next thing you know, you are being stretched again (deduct 3 points from your STAMINA). Now will you tell them the truth (turn to **256**) or claim to be a military spy (turn to **363**)?

137

The man wearing close-fitting black garments has a young yet leathery face and close-cropped hair. He shouts with a consuming anger: 'We waste too much time trying to appease our neighbours. It was they who started the War of the Four Kingdoms, yet it is we who must go crawling to them for trade. We should seize what is rightfully ours. Now our great nation is eclipsed by the barbaric Femphrey. We are clearly superior and would have won the war, were it not for that old fool Tantalon who sold us, his people, down the river. Traitor! We must demand recompense or take it for ourselves from Brice, Femphrey and those rats in the north. Northlanders and sorcerers! Pah! The enemy within. We want to be proud of Gallantaria again. We want war!'

This agitator is cruel and narrow-minded – and yet, unbelievably, some of the people seem to be nodding at his words of blind hatred. Someone must take a stand against him. Will you argue with the agitator (turn to **205**) or silence him with your fists (turn to **149**)?

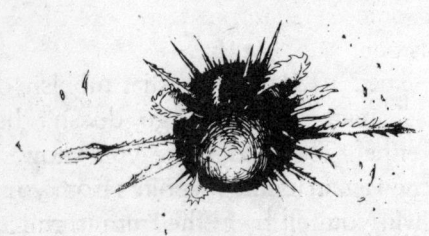

138

Feeling smug, you challenge the clown to a friendly game of dice. She agrees, and a small crowd gathers to watch you thrash the living daylights out of her. Though she manages to maintain her smile, you sense her anger. She pushes, prods and twists the loaded die in a bid to discover its mechanism, but fails.

Eventually, she concedes, 'An obvious trick, but the punters should be deceived by it.' Turn to **77**.

139

If this is your first time here, turn to **308**. If it is not your first time here, things are as you left them, and you will have to retrace your steps back to the junction. There, you may turn either to the left (turn to **217**) or to the right (turn to **296**), or continue straight on, out of the caves (turn to **80**).

140

Bartolph squirms in fear as you crush his wrist in a grip of iron; but when you call him a cheat, he reacts with outrage. Although you're not sure whether or not this 'anger' is merely the art of a practised con-man, the performance seems to work.

A number of onlookers step forward, 'You lost fair 'n' square,' snarls one.

'No place for bad losers in 'ere,' grunts another.

Before you know it, you are seized by a dozen strong hands and thrown out into the street. You land flat on your face, hitting the dirty cobbles with a painful thud (deduct 1 STAMINA point and cross off from your *Adventure Sheet* the gold you lost).

Overcome with anger, you consider drawing your sword and going back into the inn to deal with the lot of them. But then again... Turn to **30**.

141

The tower is cracked and worn with age, its once bright colours faded and peeled. There is only a single entrance, a door on which a brass plaque is fixed, engraved with the following words: 'Dr Kauderwelsch – Diseases of the Mind'. You try to open the door but it is locked. Hanging at one side is a small bell-pull. Will you ring the bell (turn to **281**) or leave the tower and head into town (turn to **212**)?

142

Sounds of battle come from the town as the people of Hustings defend their homes against the slaughtering Haggwort fiends. You ignore the din as you reach the foot of the pinnacle – and walk right into an ambush. A door opens in the side of the pinnacle and six Haggwort appear. They seize you and drag you up a long spiral stairway which ends in a small room at the top of the tower. One end of the room is closed off by heavy drapes.

If you have a weapon, cross it off your *Adventure Sheet* – the Haggwort have just broken it! They force you to sit down at a table, on which rest a sharpened wooden stake and a plate. The Haggwort mutely motion you to eat the 'food' on the plate: a mound of wet sludge. Will you eat the food (turn to **61**) or refuse (turn to **359**)?

143

Roggmondo's face is impassive as he gestures towards a big leather chair in the middle of the room. Fixed to one of the arms of the chair is a small tray holding all the pins and dyes that Roggmondo uses in his work. You settle down in the seat and Roggmondo shows a book filled with stylish pictures and designs which range from the everyday to the exotic. Suddenly the door bursts open and five city guards rush in, swords drawn. You are caught sitting down. The captain shouts triumphantly through his helmet, 'Gotcha!' Turn to **199**.

144

Descending a long, wide staircase, you come to a crossroads. A strange fire burns you (deduct 1 point from your STAMINA). Will you go:

North?	Turn to **106**
South?	Turn to **187**
East?	Turn to **122**
West?	Turn to **253**

145

You run to the meeting place and are pleased to find Mendokan and his two friends waiting for you. One of them is very old, making the ensuing journey painfully slow. To make up for this, you have to walk long into the night and are all very tired when you reach the Magyaar Pass. This, the narrowest stretch of the Trade Route, is little more than a rocky path. On the left looms a sheer rock-face, and on the right runs a deep crevice, about six metres wide and five times that deep. On the far side of the crevice is another path. By common agreement, all traffic from Lendle uses the path you are on, while all traffic going to Lendle uses the far path. As you walk through the pass, the Magyaar Walls blot out the moonlight and the shining stars above.

Suddenly, a dreadful cry pierces the air, followed by another, and another. The villagers cringe in terror, while you prepare for combat. Then you see them, coming along the path towards you: five riders on hellish steeds whose hoofs make the very earth quake, and who race to crush you underfoot. Their robes billow and their long hair flows in the wind. Even though they wear strange metallic masks, you can see that their skin is decayed and their eyes are black bottomless pits of death. Mendokan wails, 'We are doomed. The Shadow Warriors are upon us!' The others run, but their flight is a futile one; they are swiftly put to the sword. But the Warriors, they are real after all! Will you stand and fight them (turn to **190**) or admit that you cannot hope to fend off all five united, and flee (turn to **28**)?

146

You maintain a dignified yet stubborn silence. The shaman laughs and dances as the torturer cranks the handle on the stretch rack yet again (deduct 3 more points from your STAMINA). 'Are you stoopid or summat?' asks Uggamonggo. 'If yoo wanna see tomorrer, yoo'd better talk fast (turn to **198**), but if yoo wanna die, just carry on keepin' yer gob shut (turn to **269**).'

147

Lying on the desk you find a freshly written document – the ink on the vellum page is still wet. You read the text: it is copied in a hand which grows increasingly spidery and fraught:

The Dream Circus has come to Royal Lendle. This innocuous-seeming little troupe has spread its evil for over a year now, passing from village to village across Gallantaria unaware that I have been keeping a watch on its movements, awaiting the moment to act. The plan is clever. I can only hope to uncover its architect before matters come to a head. Wait! My door opens and three Circus people enter. They know, they know! The Mandrakes. Must conjure fire to destr

The letter ends suddenly. Now the mystery is less so. These Mandrakes, whatever they are, must have taken or destroyed the magician – but, to do that, they must be incredibly powerful. You have stumbled on the edges of a vast plot. Add Hegmar's Warning to your

Adventure Sheet. Now you can either examine the sarcophagus (turn to **193**) or the crystal sphere (turn to **312**), if you have not already done so; or you can leave the building (turn to **216**).

148

'Well, that can easily be arranged,' she snarls as she kicks you off your high seat. You fall down on to the dusty road, twisting your ankle (deduct 2 points from your STAMINA). When you look up, you see that all the circus performers have climbed down from their wagons and are coming after you! The clown smiles as you run for your life. If you have a set of Calthrops, you throw them in the performers' way. They will soon give up the chase and continue on their journey south. Erase the Calthrops from your *Adventure Sheet* and turn to **9**. If you don't have any Calthrops (or do not wish to use them), turn to **91**.

149

Sickened by the blackguard's venom, you step forward and lay him flat with a single punch. While many of the onlookers gasp in surprise, four of them shout, 'Brice-loving dog!' You realize that they must be followers of the man you have just hit, trouble-making agitators who are skilled at whipping up crowds into outbursts of senseless violence. Indeed, it takes the men only a minute to begin a mass brawl. The unrest is growing ugly and the city guards are hard pressed to restore order. Will you join in and help them defeat the trouble-makers (turn to **181**), or use the confusion to slip away towards the city's East Gate (turn to **301**)?

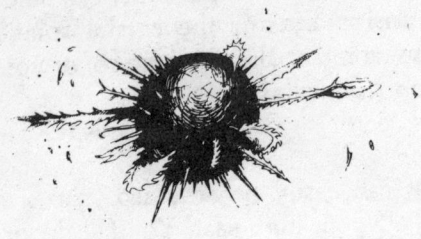

150

You hurry back out into the hall before the cultists, coming out of the secret passage, see you. Back in the hall, will you now go north (turn to **374**), east (turn to **89**), or west (turn to **56**)? Whichever way you go, you dare not risk returning here again — because of the Dark Elves. Note on your *Adventure Sheet* that you may not choose **68** again.

151

Your money disappears into the gambler's pocket via a hand that looks like a vulture's claw (deduct the gold from your *Adventure Sheet*). Bartolph beams and says, 'You played well, but Sindla was against you. However, lest you start crying into your beer, the ever fair and selfless Bartolph will give you a chance to win your money back, and more besides — provided you can afford a stake high enough to cover your losses. What's more, this time I'll make it even easier for you. The rules are as before, but now you need roll only 3 or above to win. Are you game?' If you want to play again, turn to **94**; but if you would rather leave, turn to **30**.

152

Clouds of dust and fragments of sandstone fly through the air, obscuring the skeleton as it stretches out to destroy you. You will need Osmani, god of mercenaries, on your side for this fight. If you have already put manacles on the hands of the skeleton, you may subtract 2 from its SKILL score.

PAN-TERRIC BEHEMOTH   SKILL 11

Your blows will not harm the creature; you need to smash its skull, so, at the end of each round (whether you win the round or not), roll one die. If you roll a 6, you succeed and should turn at once to **329**. If you roll any other number, you miss the skull and must fight another round as normal.

153

You watch in horrified fascination as the weird device shakes the ground more violently. A building behind you collapses, showering you with bricks. Roll one die to see how many bricks hit you. Each hit means you have to lose 2 points from your STAMINA – though armour will take the hits first.

Wulf hurries over and frees you from the rubble. 'It's no use,' he says grimly. 'It's the witch! She has powers we cannot hope to understand. We must flee, along the southern road.' Will you go with Wulf (turn to **25**), or leave him and go to settle the score with this 'witch' (turn to **142**)?

154

You have not gone more than two metres when the Slygore spits a gout of black pus at you. The gel splashes, gurgling, on your back, where it burns and hisses. Despite yourself, you scream and fall to your knees (deduct 3 points from your STAMINA). The Slygore lurches towards your pain-racked form. You must ignore the agony you are in and leap aside before the monstrosity smothers you. *Test your Skill*. If you succeed, turn to **250**; if you fail, turn to **365**.

155

Ignoring the terrifying hissing sounds, you go quickly through all the things lying scattered about the room. The only item of interest is a Copper Key, which you may take. Then, finally, panic overtakes you and you rush back to the junction. An inexplicable fear stops you from entering this room ever again (note on your *Adventure Sheet* that you may not turn to **296** again).

Back at the junction, you may either go to the left (turn to **139**), go to the right, which will take you back out of the caves (turn to **80**), or go straight ahead (turn to **217**).

156
'Disappointing,' is all the old man says as he disappears into thin air. There is nothing for you to do but return to the hallway, and then go through either the south door (turn to **68**), the north door (turn to **374**), or the west door (turn to **56**).

157
Reluctant to step into the dank chamber, you lean over the gilt-edged mirror-frame and lash out at the parts of the pod that are within your reach.

Your blows have no effect, however. If you want to risk touching the extended mesh of veins, turn to **371**. Otherwise, you will have to leave: return to **255** and pick an option you have not already chosen.

158

Relieved, the woman leads you further down the alley. When your eyes get used to the darkness, you can make out that the woman is in a sorry state indeed: her clothes are filthy and tattered, and there is a madness in her eyes. She mumbles, 'They came seven days ago, and they left this morning. You're a stranger. You're strong. They're taking over. You can't kill them. Soon they'll come for me. And for you too, unless you do something. Perhaps you can beat them, the Mandrakes. Taking our places.' Her words tumble out in a repetitive, almost insane babble. Then she stops.

She is looking over your shoulder, back up to the entrance to the alley where a finely attired young man is standing. He smiles and extends his hand. 'Welcome, stranger. I am Ennian, the Burgomeister. Ah, I see you've been forced to listen to the ramblings of the town idiot. The old fool's been hopelessly insane for years.' You look back towards the wretched woman. Seeing the doubt growing in your eyes, she gasps, 'A mirror... do you have a mirror?' If you have a mirror, turn to **362**. If you do not, turn to **174**.

159

At the far side of the square a commotion suddenly breaks out: folk are screaming and running in all directions and, cutting a bloody path through them and towards you, is a mounted Shadow Warrior! You must defend yourself. Roll one die to see which of the Warriors you must face. When you are told to continue your adventure after defeating the Warrior, you will have to leave Shattuck before the other Warriors arrive. They are coming up the Main Trade Route, so you will either have to cross a bridge to the east (turn to **334**), or take a little-used path which leads south-westwards through the mountains (turn to **48**). Now roll:

1	Turn to **8**
2	Turn to **394**
3	Turn to **259**
4	Turn to **183**
5	Turn to **245**
6	Roll again

160

After some time, you come to a fork in the road. If you wish to keep going westwards, turn to **96**. If you take the branch to the south-east, turn to **135**.

161

What follows next is too horrific to contemplate. Urtha just laughs as you follow the ritual laid down by the folklore of ages. She even tells one of the Haggwort to obey your commands. You order it to decapitate her and then to throw both her head and her body out of the open arch window. In seconds the dreadful deed is done and Urtha's remains are consigned to the stormy skies. Pausing for a moment to regain your wits, you turn to leave — only to find Urtha standing in your way! 'I told you, I am *beyond* undeath. I suppose it was expecting too much for you to understand. Now, enough of these games.'

It looks as if your time is up. Will you attack her (turn to **305**), throw a vial of Metal Rot – if you have one – at her iron band (turn to **83**) or try to escape (turn to **221**)?

162

'I don't believe it!' Bartolph gasps in an irritating display of mock surprise. 'Even at such odds, you've lost again.' Once more, your stake is pocketed with amazing speed (deduct the gold from your *Adventure Sheet*). Then, with feigned concern, Bartolph says, 'Oh, now I feel truly guilty. Look, I'll give you one last chance. Rules as before, but now all you have to do is roll a 2 or higher. What d'you say?'

Will you accept Bartolph's final challenge (turn to **13**) or leave the tavern feeling bitter, impoverished and out of luck (turn to **30**)?

163

The words of the merchant who sold you the cloak spring to mind: 'Fine though the garment may be, 'tis best used in the hours of darkness.' At this very moment you are trying to hide in an exposed place, beneath the all-revealing light of a blazing sun. *Test your Luck*. If you are Lucky, turn to **176**; if you are Unlucky, turn to **35**.

164

Rather than climb over the low wall, you hurry through a wrought-iron gate which is decorated with shapes like falling leaves. Inside, the grass is luscious and the trees still fruitful, even though harvest-time was two months ago. Outside the gate, the guards have stopped their pursuit; they stand and watch you escape with fear and frustration. Ahead of you is a small, plain building: this is the Temple of Geomancers, the earth-priesthood who worship Titan. The Geomancers respect nature in all its forms; they are a powerful and mysterious force in Royal Lendle, much resented for their independence from the law of the land. Your plan is to reach the streets beyond the temple grounds; but you are dismayed to see that your way is blocked by a tall fence dividing the estate into two halves. The only way through this fence is via another wrought-iron gate. Its two handles are fixed on to ornate plaques, one plaque representing the sun, the other the moon. Words have been worked into the top of the gate, forming a riddle; they read: 'Reflector and reflected, one obscures the other for entry.' Will you turn the handle in the sun (turn to **254**) or the handle in the moon (turn to **264**)?

165

'I'm flattered by your interest in our humble little entourage,' she smiles. 'The Circus of Dreams has been in existence for three years, spending the first two in unappreciated poverty. But last year we had a change of ownership, and with it came an improvement in quality. The last twelve months have been most successful, with the circus spreading its own particular brand of entertainment across Gallantaria. Having played the villages, we are now moving on to the towns. One day, we hope to play the Court in Royal Lendle itself.' The clown's itinerary sounds more like a war-plan than a touring schedule to you. 'We could use someone like you,' she muses. 'Maybe you'd like to join the circus permanently?' Will you answer yes (turn to **148**) or no (turn to **103**)?

166

Balanced on the top of the door was an anti-theft device: a full chamber pot, which has just emptied its reeking contents all over you! The tin bowl itself hits you on the head. Deduct 1 point from your STAMINA and 1 point from your LUCK for this mishap. You recover, look around and discover that you are in an old lady's living-room. She jumps up from her rocking-chair and screams, 'Burglars! Robbers! Help, help!'

The city guards will not be slow in answering her cries. Will you go on through a closed door leading to the rear of the house (turn to **328**), or up a rickety staircase, leading to the first floor (turn to **292**)?

167

The creature's body thrashes wildly as you bind two of its immensely strong wrists together. Then it is fully awake. Each Attack Round, all four of its unfettered arms attack you at the same time (each with a SKILL score of 8), but you may strike back against only one of them, as if fighting four separate opponents. If you win against any of its other arms, your blows have no effect, serving only as parries. Your work is cut out for you as you face one of the ancient Kalundai.

KALUNDAI   SKILL 8   STAMINA 20

If you win, turn to **320**.

168

It takes you all your strength to escape the grip of the mire, but at last you are free. Your already sodden clothes are now caked with swamp mud. But dirt is the least of your troubles; the Haggwort are converging on the beleaguered town. Will you make for Hustings (turn to **367**) or the strange tower (turn to **142**); or do you prefer to continue across the moorland (turn to **69**)?

169

Descending a long, wide staircase, you come to a crossroads. A strange fire burns you (deduct 1 point from your STAMINA). Will you go:

North?	Turn to **106**
South?	Turn to **266**
East?	Turn to **122**
West?	Turn to **144**

170

You reach into your pack and take out a skin of oil (cross it off your *Adventure Sheet*). You are still trying to set the oil alight when the Slygore spits a quivering gout of liquid black mess at you. The sticky, gurgling sludge hits your side and burns you (deduct 3 points from your STAMINA). You scream, but manage to throw the now-blazing oil all over the abominable creature. Though the fire causes Slygore's bubbling skin to gurgle more rapidly, it seems to have no adverse effect; it does, however, make the creature pause in its tracks. You seize the opportunity to turn tail and flee. Turn to **180**.

171

Holding the Spear of Doom up high, you shout your war-cry and charge. The Spear is not meant to kill Voivod; as the Horned God said, it returns life to the dead. But Voivod is death itself, so the Spear may not have enough Life-force to affect him. Fight each Attack Round of combat as normal; but once, at the end of each round (whether you win the round or not), you can attempt to give Voivod life. Roll two dice: if the total rolled is equal to or less than the Spear's current Life-force, turn to 400; but if the number you roll is higher, you have failed. If you fail, deduct 1 point from the Spear's Life-force, then fight another round of combat, and so on. Because you are trying to wield the Spear, you fight Voivod only in defence: if you *win* a round, he loses no STAMINA; on the other hand, Voivod thrives on your death, so if you *lose* a round, you must add any points of STAMINA that you lose to Voivod's current total. If the Spear expends its Life-force, you must try to defeat the Voivod in normal combat — only then will your telling blows cause him to lose STAMINA points.

VOIVOD   SKILL 10   STAMINA 10

Should it be that you win in normal combat, turn to 303.

172

At last you are free from this accursed nightmare — for nightmare it was! You walked down the staircase only once before being sent into a deep sleep by the Nightmare Master, the *true* Guardian of the Gateway. Since then, everything has been a dream, with you repeatedly walking down the same staircase. You would have done so for all eternity, had you not had the strength of will to escape. When you wake up, at the foot of the stairs, you see that you are actually inside a hellish chamber. And in it stands your foe, the Nightmare Master, surrounded by the tormented wails of the many souls still lost in his evil dreamworld. The Guardian attacks you without mercy, and his mystic weapons have the power to blight your fate. Each time you lose an Attack Round, you must deduct 1 point from your LUCK, whether you lose STAMINA or not.

NIGHTMARE MASTER   SKILL 9   STAMINA 9

If you win, turn to **361**.

173

You ask the lady who she is. She replies, 'Is it important?' You reply that it is. At this, she stares at you intently and asks, 'And how long have you had this need to identify things?' You have had enough of this stupidity. You strongly advise her to tell you who she is, but she just rushes out of the room.

You follow her up a short staircase and into the highest room in the tower: a laboratory packed with all sorts of chilling apparatus. The lady dabbles in the worst sorceries, and her latest project is lumbering towards you. It is a mish-mash of surgically joined body-parts. The woman laughs at your horrified face and rants, 'My creation may not be a pretty sight, but it is highly functional. All it needs now is an excellent brain... your brain! Yes *I* am Doktor Kauderwelsch.' The monster steps forward to kill you.

KAUDERWELSCH MONSTER
SKILL 8   STAMINA 14

If you win, turn to **87**.

174

You don't understand the woman's odd request and don't have a mirror anyway, so you just shrug your shoulders in uncertainty. Frustrated and no longer able to contain her fears, the woman runs off towards the far end of the alleyway. The Burgomeister calls over his shoulder for some help, then laughs, 'Not the best company for a stranger to keep! It must all seem a tad peculiar, but everything will make perfect sense if you'll just come with me.' All your instincts scream that there is something terribly wrong here. Will you attack the Burgomeister (turn to **252**), make for the other end of the alley after the woman (turn to **84**), or comply with Ennian's wishes and go with him (turn to **31**)?

175

Your skin prickles and it feels as if a knife is being twisted in your gut when Bartolph leans forward and thrusts his ruddy, laughing face mere inches away from your own. 'I'm sorry, but that's it now. I won't play with losers – after all, I do have to sleep at nights. The game is over.' Deduct the gold you have lost from your *Adventure Sheet* — Bartolph has added it to his already considerable winnings. Feeling somehow as if you've been taken for a ride, you get up and walk out of the First Step. Turn to **30**.

176

Hugging the ground, you cannot help but think that, for once, a trader at Royal Lendle has sold his merchandise short. The Chameleon Cloak works its wonders as you sneak away beneath the smelly Orcs' very noses and escape.

However, you are now forced to leave the road and cut south over the difficult mountain terrain, where progress is slow. After a few hours of hard slog, you find a small mine shaft. It goes down fifteen metres or so before ending in an illuminated chamber of some sort. The narrowness of the shaft prevents you from seeing the nature of the place. If you have a rope and grapple, you may use it to climb down the shaft (turn to **383**). If you do not have, or do not wish to use, any rope you will have to continue your journey over the mountains (turn to **282**).

177

While you are looking in your pack for something to give the scoundrel, it suddenly occurs to you that you may be able to give him something which could prove his undoing. If you want to give the highwayman a Chameleon Cloak, turn to **220**. If you would rather give him an Orb of Mind-snaring, turn to **128**. But if you have neither of these things, you will either have to offer him some gold (turn to **373**) or attack him (turn to **92**).

178
You step quietly up to the shelter and reach for the door handle. As soon as you touch it, the door swings outwards, propelled by three powerful springs. *Test your Luck*. If you are Lucky, turn to **64**; if you are Unlucky, turn to **342**.

179
The big top is lantern-lit and lined with rows of seats in readiness for tonight's performance. As you look at the circus ring, the main pole, the trapeze, the tightrope, you feel a mild headache rising behind your eyes. If you have a mirror, turn to **268**. If you do not, there is nothing more for you to do here. It does occur to you, however, that the secret of the circus is most likely to be found in the Hall of Dreams. Return to **255** and choose an option you have not picked before.

180
As you turn away from the Slygore, it spits a blob of acidic black pus at your face. You manage to duck just in time. The squeaking lump of muck flies over your head and embeds itself in a sewer wall, turning brick into dripping clay. Not waiting to see what the creature will do next, you run for your life. With a great splash, the Slygore drops its awesome body into the foul waters and rushes after you. Soon, with sinking heart you come to a dead end – and then you spot a ladder

leading back up to the surface! From above come the faint voices of city guards looking for you. Behind you, the Slygore raises itself up once more, its foul mass now revealed by the light coming through an overhead grid ... The sight is one you will never forget. Will you now clamber up out of the sewer (turn to **18**), or turn and embrace the creature in close combat (turn to **365**)?

181

You see that you can do most good by defeating the toughest of the agitators. This huge brute is cutting a swath of blood through bystanders and city guards alike. There is no room for mercy with such villains!

AGITATOR   SKILL 8   STAMINA 7

If you win, turn to **370**.

182

Your foot lands less than a finger's width away from the insidious artefact. What with the quicksand, the

Haggwort and now these evil traps, the moors are just too dangerous. You decide to leave them at once. If you want to go to the town, turn to **367**. If you would rather investigate the mysterious tower, turn to **142**.

183

This Shadow Warrior wields a mighty, multi-headed mace: each of its steel faces is covered with pyramid-shaped spikes. In the Warrior's hands, the mace is a devastating weapon. At the start of the battle, *Test your Luck*. If you are Lucky, nothing untoward happens; if you are Unlucky, however, the mace smashes your weapon and you must fight without it (cross the weapon off your *Adventure Sheet*). If you have no weapon, the mace crashes into your body and you must deduct 6 points from your STAMINA and 1 point from your SKILL. Armour or *Testing your Luck* may not be used to reduce this damage.

Fourth SHADOW WARRIOR   SKILL 9   STAMINA 9

If you defeat the Warrior, turn to **335**.

184

You put on a final spurt so that you will reach the South Gate well ahead of the mob. Just as you thought: a Mandrake stands guard. From what you have already seen, these creatures are good fighters and are impossible to kill. Though you could stun the guard, a fight would be time-consuming, giving the mob a chance to catch up with you. It would be far better if you could sneak up on the guard and somehow render him harmless without having to resort to combat. If you have some manacles and would like to try to bind the guard with them, turn to **319**. If you don't have any manacles or would rather risk combat anyway, turn to **55**.

185

The skeleton stirs and drags itself free from the layers of rock. And a nightmarish roar rises from its rib-cage — as new flesh appears and starts to crawl back over its bones! The beast is re-forming before your very eyes. Only one creature could possibly do this, a thing which also has the power of mind-control! Now you know why you strayed off the road to Karnstein, now you know why Guignol's expedition found exactly what it was looking for in the endless wilderness, now you understand the reason for everything that has happened here. You were all drawn here and controlled by a fierce intelligence that plotted its own release. Only now do you realize that you are facing a creature from mythology: a Pan-Terric Behemoth! You must destroy it before it is whole again. The only way to do so is by smashing its skull. If you have a rope and grapple, you may try to snare the creature; *Test your Skill*. If you succeed, turn to **329**. But if you fail, or if you do not have a rope and grapple, turn to **152**.

186

You wake up, bound to a table in a laboratory, in the topmost room of the Cumbleside tower. The lady you met earlier walks into view, clutching a scalpel! Her skin is peeling, revealing an underlayer of scales. As if in answer to your questioning stare, she says, 'I am Doktor Kauderwelsch. In my quest for immortality, I made the mistake of experimenting with lizard organisms which, even now, are taking me over. I will die unless I find a way to transfer my mind into another body. And you are a vital part in my most crucial experiment to date. Behold!' She waves an arm and a horrible monster lumbers forward. 'I have created this being from the finest parts of many creatures. All it needs now is a brain – your brain!' Kauderwelsch cackles madly, scalpel raised, and the mindless monster looks as if it's about to strangle you. You quickly free one of your arms, but you have time to reach for only one item; will it be your weapon (turn to **242**), a mirror (turn to **318**) or a Fire-cracker (turn to **125**)? If you have none of these things, your adventure ends here, in the advancement of science!

187

Descending a long, wide staircase, you come to a crossroads. A strange fire burns you (deduct 2 points from your STAMINA). Will you go:

North?	Turn to **106**
South?	Turn to **114**
East?	Turn to **232**
West?	Turn to **253**

188

If you allowed yourself to be diverted and gambled with Bartolph in the First Step tavern, turn to **321**. If you did not, you may continue on your way. If you are heading east, turn to **82**; if you are heading west, turn to **66**.

189

Voivod is about to toll the Iron Bell. If you have a vial of Metal Rot and want to throw it at the bell, turn to **263**. If you haven't any Metal Rot, but are willing to try a desperate leap, in a bid to knock Voivod away from the bell, turn to **348**. If, however, you wish to do neither of these things, turn to **364**.

190

Though you attack with all your might, you are defenceless against the onslaught of the malevolent riders. They cut you and knock you fiercely to the ground (deduct 4 points from your STAMINA). Lying on the cold earth, it seems that you have three options: to stay where you are and pretend to be dead (turn to **306**), to rise and fight them again (turn to **346**) or to jump to your feet and flee (turn to **28**).

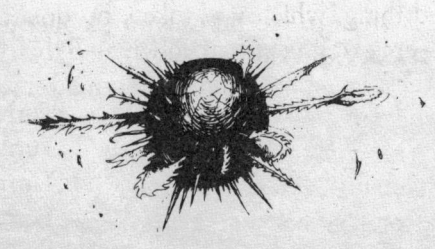

191

The floor drops away beneath your feet, and you go tumbling down into a deep pit (deduct 1 point from your STAMINA). If you have a rope and grapple, turn to **124**; otherwise, turn to **336**.

192

You hide the Dark Elves' bodies under the table, then pause for thought. It would take hours just to find out what all the different scrolls and books are about, and time is short. So you content yourself with a brief look at those texts which the cultists were perusing. Will you read the *Numeris Astrakkaans* (turn to **366**) or the *Ur-Mythalia* (turn to **79**)?

193

The burial casket is old beyond reckoning, and its wood is primitively carved in the shape of a bestial warrior. You pull open the cover of the sarcophagus with great care and step in. It is only when the lid clicks shut that the trap is sprung, however! Two sharp blades flick inwards from the sides of the casket, cutting into your calves and ankles (deduct 1 point from your STAMINA and 1 point from your SKILL). In pain, you free yourself and kick the lid open; you stumble out of this wretched thing, which was taken, no doubt, from the tomb of some king who had anticipated the coming of treasure-seeking grave-robbers. To add insult to injury, you now see, too late, that the carving on the lid has no feet. You curse yourself for missing this sickly humorous clue. Now will you examine the crystal orb (turn to **312**) or Hegmar's desk (turn to **147**), if you have not done so already; or will you leave this place before worse befalls you (turn to **216**)?

194

You walk over to the cool waters and are about to drink when you hear a stern voice call, 'Stand and deliver!' You turn around and find yourself facing a masked highwayman; he is aiming a crossbow at your heart. The villain laughs. 'No doubt you're another fool in search of the hermit. Well, forget it. He's dead, and I killed him. And I'll do the same to you unless you can buy your freedom.' His finger tightens on the trigger of the crossbow.

Will you attack the knave (turn to **92**), offer him some gold (turn to **373**), or look in your pack for something else to give him (turn to **177**)?

195

'You're quite right,' you reply to the Man-Orc with a sickly smile. 'It *is* none of my business, and I apologize.' The Orc is astonished by this sudden turn of events, and he doesn't know what is going on when you pat him on the shoulder with one hand and slip the Sleeping Draught into his drink with the other. The bewildered Orc takes a big gulp from his tankard ... then falls flat on his face! Turn to **120**.

196

Your prospects of reaching the East Gate are soon dashed when you see that the pathway ends in a high, locked door. This door is too strong to be knocked down and too smooth to be climbed, so you will have to try and jump over it. If you wish to attempt such a difficult feat, turn to **52**. Otherwise, you will have to go back up the alley and face any guards who may have followed you down it; turn to **20**.

197

The whole circus becomes one great funeral pyre. You stand and watch as the flames leap high into the sky. The stench of Mandrakes burning is indescribable! As you look on, Jack-in-the-Green appears by your side. 'Earth-mother is pleased with her champion. She sends two gifts. The first is this . . .' He hands you a Ring of Destiny. From now on, whenever you are Lucky at *Testing your Luck*, you do not have to subtract a LUCK point. As long as you have the ring, you need only ever lose LUCK points if you are Unlucky, or if you are instructed to do so by the text. 'The second gift is knowledge. The man of numbers is a native of Shattuck.' Then the ever elusive figure is gone.

Grateful for the Earth-mother's help, you move further on and rest for the night in a quiet field. When you wake up (restore 2 STAMINA points) you make your way into Shattuck. The small town is refreshingly quiet and untroubled. You need to find this 'man of numbers', and the only way to do so is by asking around. Will you start your search in:

The stores?	Turn to **391**
The taverns?	Turn to **209**
The town square?	Turn to **27**

198

Will you tell Uggamonggo the truth, that you are a mercenary on your way to Karnstein (turn to **256**); that you're spying on the Orcs, on behalf of the king of Gallantaria (turn to **363**), or that you're not on any mission at all, that you're just a simple adventurer (turn to **136**)?

199

The city guards take you to a nearby jail, where you are to be held until dawn tomorrow. At that time, an armoured wagon will come to take you to the city dungeon – a grim complex from which very few ever return. The guards take your weapon (cross it off your *Adventure Sheet*) and lock you in a dirty cage. Then they depart, leaving you in the care of the jailer. This brute sits by a table, sucking on a bottle of grog and reading a book called *Confessions of a Rat-Catcher*. Since there is only one cage in the jail, no other prisoners and only the single jailer, your thoughts turn to escape. Luckily, none of your other possessions have been taken from you. Will you pour some Metal Rot, if you have any, on the lock and slip out (turn to **7**); shout an insult at the jailer, in the hope that he will come to punish you, thus giving you a chance to overpower him (turn to **26**); think of a way to trick the jailer into setting you free (turn to **38**), or do nothing and await the morrow's dungeon-wagon (turn to **208**)?

200

Rain pours down your face as you reach into your pack for a vial of the precious potion. The Mahogadon squeezes ever tighter and starts to pull you towards its gaping, gnashing maw. Mere inches away from certain death, you open the vial and fling its contents down into the pool of sludge that surrounds the monster's roots. Almost immediately, the Mahogadon sags, limp and unconscious. Its branches unwind and roll you away, down on to the muddy earth. The lightning no longer hounds you as you make your way out of the copse to freedom. If you now wish to continue southwards, across more open country, towards Hustings, turn to **135**. If you would prefer to head back to the safety of the road, turn to **160**.

201

Urtha smirks, then orders the Haggwort to release you. You rise from your chair and pick up the stake. Urtha rips open her costume, revealing a disgusting black hole over her heart. 'I told you,' she says. 'I have already been destroyed by the stake. By all the old laws of nature, I should not be. Your stake destroys the Undead. I am *beyond* undeath.'

If you have a vial of Metal Rot, you can now try throwing it at her iron band (turn to **83**). Otherwise you will either have to attack her (turn to **305**) or flee (turn to **221**).

202

There is no way that you can cross the chasm at this point. But to your left is a narrow passageway, plunged in total darkness. If you dare enter this corridor, turn to **283**. If you would rather go back the way you came, towards the shrieking cultists, turn to **297**.

203

Only when you hit the hard ground do you realize that you have seriously misjudged the exact location of the horse. Roll one die and deduct the number rolled from your STAMINA. Shocked by your sudden arrival from the sky, the horse bolts, leaving you in a cloud of dust. Coughing, you get up and limp out of the alley. You force your aching legs along a wide street, lined on both sides by crumbling terraced houses. A door to one of these jerks open, and an emaciated old man pops his head out. 'Psst. Oi, you! Sanctuary. I'll hide you for a Gold Piece.'

Looking ahead you can see that the street ends in a large, packed square. Will you accept the offer of refuge (turn to **344**) or ignore the beggar and head towards the busy square (turn to **225**)?

204

Was it luck or fate that guided you to that vital page in Hegmar's Sanctum? Whatever the answer, you thank Hegmar (wherever he may be) for his warning; then you take down one of the flaming torches that are fixed to the wall and use it to set the nascent Mandrake alight. A revolting smell fills the air as the pod shrivels and sizzles to its doom. You may restore 1 LUCK point for your narrow escape. There is nothing else to be done here, so return to **255** and choose an option you have not picked before.

205

You step forward and declare, 'We are at peace with the other nations of the Old World. Relations are good, trade is mutually beneficial, we learn much from one another. There is no place for such primitive ideas. In war nobody wins, but *you* don't care about the bloodshed as long as *your* malice is satisfied.'

The Ranter's surprise at being challenged turns to disgust. 'So . . . a Brice-lover, eh? Or maybe you're one of them. We don't need foreigners coming into our cities telling us how to live our lives, do we, boys?'

You notice four thugs standing near you. Though dressed in rags, they are clearly agitators. They draw their swords and come at you. Simultaneously, their leader spurs the crowd into a frenzy of hatred, and a huge brawl breaks out. Because of the crowded conditions, the agitators have to fight you one at a time.

	SKILL	STAMINA
First AGITATOR	7	4
Second AGITATOR	8	7
Third AGITATOR	6	6
Fourth AGITATOR	5	5

If you defeat them all, turn to 370.

206

Trying not to think about the possible consequences, you sprint towards the gaping cavemouth – and run slap bang into the hulking body of a Mountain Ogre!

MOUNTAIN OGRE   SKILL 9   STAMINA 11

If you win, you see that the cave is in fact the entrance to a pitch-black tunnel which leads deep into the mountains. You really do need a lantern to go any further. If you enter the tunnel with a lantern, cross one skin of oil off your *Adventure Sheet* and turn to 240. If you are foolish enough to enter the tunnel without a lantern, turn to 369. If you would rather go back outside and take your chances with the Orcs, turn to 35.

207

Shaking off Ennian's mob, you come to the ten-metre-high wall. If you have a rope and grapple, you may use it to scale the wall (turn to 300). Once on the other side, you will be able to tug the rope free quite easily. If you do not have a rope, you will have to head for the South Gate after all (turn to **184**).

208

The night passes with unbearable slowness and, thanks to your jailer's grog-drenched snores, you don't get a minute's sleep. At dawn, four city guards strip you of all your belongings, then escort you to a large, metal-walled wagon. Along with an assortment of rogues, you are then driven to the city dungeon. In this labyrinth of dank and murky chambers you are chained to a stone post and left to brood among a multitude of miserable forgotten souls. You fear that you will never see the light of day again. Even if you do, it will be far too late for you to help the people of Karnstein.

209

No one in any of the inns or taverns you call at knows anything about this 'man of numbers'. However, in the last place you enter, you may buy any number of Provisions at a cost of 2 Gold Pieces per meal. Where will you ask about the 'man of numbers' next: in the stores (turn to **391**) or the square (turn to **27**)?

210

Roll four dice and add up the numbers rolled. If the total is equal to or less than your current STAMINA score, turn to **29**. If the total is higher than your current STAMINA score, turn to **385**.

211

No sooner do you pick the object up when its sides flick open: vicious blades, piercing spikes and slicing razors spring out in all directions. *Test your Luck*. If you are Lucky, you drop the sphere before it can injure you. If you are Unlucky, roll one die to see how many of the device's deadly projections injure you. For each injury sustained, roll another die and lose that many STAMINA points.

If you are still alive, you may go either down the manhole (turn to **375**) or along the street (turn to **22**).

212

All the buildings of Cumbleside are in a poor state, their human occupants long gone, driven away by the encroaching evil of the mountains. You can't help but shiver as you walk through the dark, neglected streets. And your imagination seems to be playing tricks on you, because you keep seeing things. One minute it's a pair of mysterious eyes, the next it's a fleeting shadow. If the creatures were real, they would have no reason not to attack you. Unless they were waiting for something –

'Aiiiieeeeeeee!!!' A Shadow Warrior springs out of the shadows in front of you. Will you stand and fight (turn

to 311) or run back to the possible safety of the tower (turn to 141)?

213

Looking over the front line, you can see that six Haggwort are bringing up the rear with some sort of living device; it looks like a twitching, black tree-trunk – possibly a battering ram. You turn to ask Wulf if he knows what the thing is – and see to your horror that he is on the brink of death. The Haggwort are concentrating all their efforts against him, and he cannot bring his heavy longsword to bear in time to fend off their many blows. Mindful of the looming Haggwort device, will you:

Use this opportunity to flee?	Turn to 25
Go in search of the witch?	Turn to 142
Try to save your friend's life?	Turn to 285

214

You say to the clown, 'Although I don't have much experience as a performer, I'm willing to learn. I'll have a go at anything once.'

The clown beams, her eyes displaying malicious glee. 'Will you, indeed?' Then she breaks off, and everyone gathers around while she goes to fetch some props.

She places the head of a pantomime horse over your head; you can hardly see a thing through the holes cut in it. Then she puts three juggling balls in your hand and tells you to juggle with them. You have only just started when she grabs hold of you and starts spinning you around. As she does so, someone kicks you in the legs. Despite this obvious attempt to humiliate you, you must not drop a single ball. *Test your Skill*. If you succeed, turn to **77**. If you fail, turn to **67**.

215

Your mind races as you study the dead man's map. With a degree of common sense, you should be able to work out where Voivod is right now. Once you have done so, you will have to convert the place-name into numbers. If you know how to do this, get started straight away. When you think you have found the number, turn to it. If the entry you turn to does not make sense, you have chosen wrongly. If the entry does make sense, carry on with the adventure. Because Voivod is still making his initial preparations, you will have time to visit two places. If the first place you turn to happens to be the right one, you reach Voivod *early* (note this on your *Adventure Sheet*). If neither of the entries you turn to makes sense, or if you just don't know how to find Voivod in the first place, turn to **229**.

216

For a moment all is quiet, but the lull proves deceptive. By chance a guard catches sight of you and raises the alarm once more. After yet another sprint, you unwittingly enter a cul-de-sac. Ahead of you, bordered by a low wall, are the green and pleasant grounds of a small temple. To your left is the entrance to a narrow alleyway; this dingy path, lined on either side by lofty walls, heads in the general direction of the city's East Gate.

Will you enter the temple grounds (turn to **164**) or the pathway (turn to **196**)?

217

The murky, cramped corridor twists and turns for quite some way, before ending at a stout dungeon door. From behind this heavy portal comes the sound of hissing! If you wish to open the door, turn to **368**. If not, you must return to the junction and go either to the left, out of the caves (turn to **80**), to the right (turn to **139**), or straight on (turn to **296**).

218

Seeing you start to run, the shaman hurries forward and rips the pack from your back. She opens it and scatters your belongings all over the ground. You rush angrily towards her, but she flees. You won't have time to chase her, nor will you have time to recover all your things before your escape attempt is thwarted. You may recover any five items (in addition to any armour you are already wearing). All your Provisions count as one item, as do all your Gold Pieces. Once you have chosen which five things you want to keep, cross all the others off your *Adventure Sheet*. Worried that you may not escape, you waste no more time and start running. *Test your Luck*. If you are Lucky, turn to **350**, but if you are Unlucky, turn to **119**.

219

Hands flying in all directions, Zekareh, the beggar-prophet, proclaims the Doom of Titan: 'Woe is me, the end of the world is nigh. The very earth itself is dying, poisoned by the buried canker within, whose release is nigh. For when the five free the one, the very air itself shall vent decay and the dead shall walk. Only the Spear and the defender of the meek can save us.'

You find all these profound ramblings a little confusing and repetitive, so you move on. As you go, Zekareh's eye stares at you. If you have not already done so, will you now approach the young woman (turn to **289**) or the man in black (turn to **137**)?

220

'My, my. Such a fine garment. It should make my job all the easier,' laughs the robber as he snatches the cloak from you. He puts it on and becomes all but invisible in the shady clearing. You curse your own stupidity, as his voice starts to come at you from all directions: 'Begone, you miserable coward, before I lose my patience!' Try as you may, you cannot see your evil opponent, so you hurry out of the glade, away from the Wizard's Well and the highwayman's taunting. If you wish to continue northwards in search of the 'dead' hermit, turn to **349**. If you feel that you have wasted too much time already and would be better off heading back south, turn to **44**.

221

The Haggwort are blocking the stairway, so you will have to leap through the open window. A thirty-metre drop awaits you on the other side, but it is either that or certain death. If you are having second thoughts and would rather risk combat, turn to **305**. Otherwise, *Test* *your Luck* and *Test your Skill*. If you fail *either* test, you plummet to your death. If you pass *both* tests, however, you miraculously survive, with only a loss of 2 STAMINA points.

Rushing through the town, you see that the Haggwort are laying it to waste and butchering those of its inhabitants who have not already fled. You too escape along the road leading south. Turn to **25**.

222

'What! I? A cheat? How dare you!' Despite the pain caused by your tight grip on his puny wrist, Bartolph is still able to put on a show of offended outrage that seems a little too well practised. As far as the onlookers can tell, you lost fair and square. When you pick up the die and roll 1 seven times in a row, however, they make it quite clear that they like cheats even less than they like bad losers. They grab Bartolph and prepare to drag him into the back yard. Before the rogue disappears altogether, you search him for any gold which you have already lost to him; in addition you take 6 Gold Pieces belonging to him. Satisfied that justice is about to be done, you close your ears to Bartolph's whining and leave the tavern, taking his die with you. Add the Gold Pieces and the Loaded Die to your *Adventure Sheet*, and turn to **30**.

223

As the defeated Shadow Warrior falls, groaning in an untidy heap, you reach forward and snatch its weird mask away from its face. The Warrior's scream slices through the air; its body dissolves in a whirlwind of crimson energy, which spins and spins until it burns out and simply fades away. Though not destroyed, the Shadow Warrior will not be seen again for a hundred years. Note on your *Adventure Sheet* which Warrior you have just banished; you will not have to face this Warrior again. If you are told that you will have to, ignore the instructions — you face nothing. If in future you roll this Warrior when you roll to see which of the five you must face, roll again until you get a different one. Now continue your adventure.

224

Smegg leads you away from the bright chamber and takes you down many a cramped and winding passageway. A short while later, you come to a small cave with a hole in the floor. 'Smeggies pit,' declares Smegg as he takes the stout rope from his shoulder. He ties a loop round his waist and then offers you the other end. 'Put rope round you. Smegg lower you down. Tunnel at bottom. Goes under Elfies.' If you want to continue along 'Smeggies route', turn to **313**. If, however, the thought of climbing down a shaft at Smegg's mercy gives you second thoughts, turn to **50**.

225

You have just entered one of Royal Lendle's major tourist attractions, Masonic Square. Filled with traders' and merchants' stalls, the major feature of its buildings is their fine stonework and the statues depicting the life of Orjan the Builder. Some say that the measurements, angles and proportions of the square hold some deep mystical significance. You, however, are more concerned with the number of city guards watching all the exits leading from it. At the moment they are not looking for you, but they soon will be, once those guards dogging your footsteps arrive. You need a diversion. If chaos were to reign – however briefly – over the hundreds of people crammed into the square, you would have no trouble slipping away. There is only one thing that could possibly cause such an uproar: gold. If you have any Gold Pieces, decide how many you wish to throw, then deduct them from your *Adventure Sheet*. Then roll one die. If the number rolled is higher than the number of Gold Pieces you have thrown, turn to **389**; if the number rolled is equal to or lower than the number of Gold Pieces you have thrown, turn to **57**. If you don't have any Gold, or choose not to waste any, you must surrender to the guards (turn to **199**).

226

Obeying your finely honed instincts, you drop to the ground and roll forward just as a cloud of knock-out gas floats through the air to where you were standing. Made wary by this trap, you leave the place and make your way around more stealthily: walking on rooftops, sneaking through backyards, never once entering a place by obvious means. In doing so, you come to learn that the whole town is just one big maze of traps. It is a miracle that you have got this far without further mishap. You decide not to push your luck too far and make your way out of town. If you want to head south, turn to **75**. If you would rather skirt back round the

town and investigate the tower you saw earlier, turn to **141**.

227

With only a brief interval for some much-needed sleep (restore 2 STAMINA points), you continue westwards until you come to the Burning Balrog Inn. The place is empty but for the landlord and three Femphrey warriors, veterans of the War of the Four Kingdoms. Judging by the noise they are making, the veterans have already had too much to drink. And if this isn't bad enough, they are sitting with a Man-Orc assassin who, seeing you, shouts, 'I fawt I cud smell sumfink. It's a Gallantreean.'

One of the veterans drawls, 'Pah, lezz kick the backstabbin' worm outta here.'

The oldest of the veterans stares at you intently, then growls, 'It *is* you! We fought in the Battle of Mallagash, and you gave me this!' He lifts up his left arm; in place of his hand is a metal hook. Now you remember: he was a sergeant-at-arms who would have killed you, but for the severe wound you inflicted on him. Stirred by the troublesome Man-Orc, the veterans are growing angrier by the second. Will you ignore them and go to the bar (turn to **3**), ask the veterans why they are with a Man-Orc (turn to **287**), or attack the assassin, before he goads the veterans on to violence (turn to **265**)?

228

Not a single one of the circus folk hears or sees you as you imitate a desert lizard and wriggle towards them.

Predictably, it is the clown who is doing most of the talking. '... as before, but not as sloppily as at Gornt. This time, we'll control the intake by keeping the circus out of town. Though Gornt will ultimately be a success, it was messy. The operation must be carried out with greater stealth, so that we can attain the monthly target figure through careful management rather than by hurried processing.'

You're not at all sure what this all means, and you don't receive any enlightenment when the conversation moves on to normal circus business. You sneak away to reconsider your options. Return to **255** and choose an option you have not selected already.

Your journey has taken too long. Perhaps you failed to take the threat of Voivod seriously enough, but the Warlord is no paltry dictator. He has already raised an army, ten thousand strong, of shambling Undead and, through his Shadow Warrior lieutenants, is masterminding an invasion of the living world. The ground writhes beneath your feet as the Earth-mother and the Horned God realize that all is lost.

230

If you have a Fire-cracker, turn to **317**. If you have a skin of oil (the lantern is not needed), turn to **170**. (If you have both, you may choose either.) If you have neither, you will have to flee: turn to **356**.

231

The further you go into the town, the more you see of its madness. Brother fighting brother, the town militia divided, houses being burned down and worse besides. Yet while half of the people seem frightened, the others seem relaxed; they smile while they fight and try to persuade their more worried opponents that they are being foolish. You decide it would be best to remain unseen, so you move about using whatever cover is available. It is while you are tiptoeing between buildings that a hand clamps over your mouth and an arm pulls you back into an alley. A woman's voice whispers, 'Hush, be still!' If you do as the woman commands, turn to **158**. If you strike out at her, turn to **129**.

232

Descending a long, wide staircase, you come to a crossroads. A strange fire burns you (deduct 3 points from your STAMINA). Will you go:

North?	Turn to **169**
South?	Turn to **187**
East?	Turn to **122**
West?	Turn to **144**

233

Quinsberry Woad sneers vindictively as his men strip you of practically all your belongings. 'Someone with your particular talents should have no trouble in recouping his losses. Failing gainful employment, you can always fall back on robbing old women.' He allows himself a petty chuckle before leading his men away with your things. 'Don't forget,' he calls, 'seven days!'

This is a most annoying and unfortunate start to your adventure. You can only hope that you will not let the people of Karnstein down any further. With nothing else to do, you make your way out of the city. Cross off everything except your weapon from your *Adventure Sheet*, and turn to **145**.

234

You try to throw yourself aside, but too late! The moment your foot touches the disc, there is an implosion of Darklight.

A moment later, when you regain consciousness, you feel nauseous but seem to be still in one piece (deduct 1 point from your STAMINA). However, the mystic snare has made some of your equipment disappear! Erase any *two* items of equipment from your *Adventure Sheet*. You may choose which items to cross off, but all your Provisions count as one item, as do all your Gold Pieces.

You no longer feel that crossing the moors is a good idea: there are too many dangers. If you want to head for the town, turn to **367**. If you would rather go and investigate the strange tower, turn to **142**.

235

Casting your doubts aside, you tuck into the meal – and soon succumb to the sleeping draught which has been sprinkled all over your food. Turn to **186**.

236

'What?' he gasps. 'Cleanliness? In Lendle? There's no such thing.' He swiftly pulls back a curtain, separating the parlour from his living quarters, and calls, 'Bransell!' In response, his pet appears: a ferocious wolf-sized rat! Before you know it, the rodent is upon you, its grasping talons clawing at your skin.

BRANSELL   SKILL 6   STAMINA 9

If you win, as you leave the parlour you grab 4 Gold Pieces from Roggmondo's till and leave the tattooist to weep over the carcass of his fallen guard-rat. Out in the street, you see a large crowd seething ahead of you, and an angry guard patrol behind. Turn to **118**.

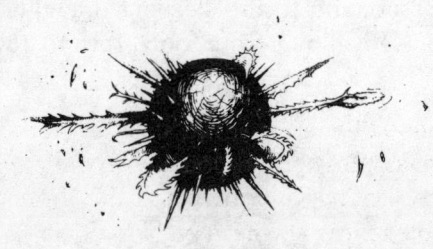

237

You step up to the statue and pour the precious drops between its petrified lips. In moments, the old scholar is flesh again. 'It cannot be . . . but it is!' he quavers. Then he pushes past you and makes his way out of the cave. His fear of being caught again is stronger than his gratitude. But his shouts have already drawn unwanted attention. Something is moving in the shadows behind the six remaining statues. If you have a mirror, turn to **322**. If you haven't, *Test your Luck*. If you are Lucky, turn to **21**; but if you are Unlucky, turn to **34**.

238

To your amazement, you land squarely on the horse's back. However, the impact proves to be quite painful (deduct 1 point from your STAMINA). Up on the roof, the city guards watch dumbfounded as you urge the horse out of the alley and away. You stop for nothing, speeding through crowded squares and alleyways towards the city's North Gate. There, you dismount and send the horse home with a good slap. You cannot resist a quiet chuckle as you walk past the gate wardens who, ignorant of your misdemeanours, merely stand by as you exit the city. Turn to **145**.

239

You unhook the lanterns and spill oil on the seats, over the canvas, down the ropes, everywhere. Then you fling the flaming lanterns on to the ground and soon the whole tent is aflame. You hurry outside and almost run into the circus folk, standing before you, Mandrakes hissing their hatred. For a moment you think you are done for, but no. The Mandrakes merely stand their ground. Then you notice the nervous look on the clown's face. Her eyes glance over your shoulder, looking behind you at the tent, at the fire. That's it – the Mandrakes' one weakness must be fire! Will you use this special knowledge to attack the Mandrakes (turn to **17**) or use the fire as a diversion and flee (turn to **104**)?

240

You follow endless kilometres of underground passages, your internal sense of direction ensuring that you are always heading roughly southwards. The corridor you are currently following seems to end in a room with phosphorescent walls. Facing you, at the far end of this room, is an open arch, beyond which is a descending staircase. A strange-shaped metal plate hangs over the archway. You are still approaching the room when you see something stir in the darkness on the very threshold of the chamber. In a high voice, the silhouette calls out, 'Halt! Me Smegg, Guardian of the Gate.' As you draw closer to the figure, you see that it is a small humanoid, clad in the skin of his latest conquest – a giant spider! Suppressing your revulsion, will you do as Smegg commands and stay where you are (turn to **95**), or do you attack him (turn to **50**)?

241

Years of separation have made your partnership with your old friend a little rusty; you move too slowly to dodge the deadly sharp machete which sinks into your shoulder (deduct 3 points from your STAMINA). If you are still alive, you straighten up as Villgran pulls the weapon out and throws it aside. Thanking the old man, you turn to see Wulf kill the very Haggwort who just threw the machete at you. Will you:

Rush over to the barricade?	Turn to **298**
Go to confront the witch?	Turn to **142**
Flee from Hustings before worse befalls you?	Turn to **25**

242

It is difficult, but not impossible, to defend yourself from the monster while unbuckling the straps which bind you to the table. However, you must subtract 1 point from your Attack Strength for the first five rounds of combat – the time it takes you to free yourself. Kauderwelsch stands back, cackling insanely.

KAUDERWELSCH MONSTER

SKILL 8   STAMINA 14

If you win, turn to **87**.

243

Your hasty search turns up 1 Gold Piece on the corpse of one of the thugs – the measly sum Bartolph paid them to kill you! You may take this coin in the brief second that passes before the guards appear and throw a weighted net at you. You will have to leap aside before you are snared like a cornered rat. *Test your Skill*. If you succeed, you dodge the net and may run up the street (turn to **360**) or further down the alley (turn to **262**). If you fail, you are entangled and captured (turn to **199**).

244

While Bonesquagg Grogmaker's not looking, you take a vial of the potent draught and pour it into the bubbling cauldron of cockroach and rat-droppings stew! Knowing humans' fussy tastes, none of the Orcs is suspicious when you politely decline a bowl of the stuff; and it only takes ten minutes for the draught to do its work. Soon the whole area echoes to the rumble of Orcish snoring. Restore 1 point of LUCK for your clever planning. Rummaging through the Orcs' belongings, you find a sword and two (barely edible) meals of Provisions, which you may take. Then you flee along a rugged mountain track. *Test your Luck*. If you are Lucky, turn to **350**. If you are Unlucky, turn to **119**.

245

This Shadow Warrior carries a number of deadly throwing stars which are cast in a magical substance called Cruel-metal. Any wounds caused by the metal keep growing – tearing and splitting the body until the victim suffers a slow and painful death. At the start of your battle, the Warrior will have time to spin one such missile in your direction. *Test your Skill*. If you succeed, you dodge the star and begin combat as normal; but if you fail, the star embeds itself deep within your body, and you die in seconds.

Fifth SHADOW WARRIOR   SKILL 9   STAMINA 9

If you defeat the Warrior, turn to **335**.

246

Roll one die: the number you roll tells you the number of attempts you may make to cut the ropes before the Dark Elves will reach you. You must roll 9 or above with two dice, in order to succeed. If you don't have a weapon, you must subtract 1 from your rolls. If you succeed in cutting the ropes inside the allotted number of tries, turn to **261**. If you don't manage it, turn to **309**.

247

A few hours pass; you find yourself in a wide, open field when the overcast sky breaks to the sound of thunder and is torn apart by jagged lightning. Soon you are drenched in torrents of rain. In the near distance, to your right, is a copse which may offer some shelter. Straight ahead are more open fields. You are just wondering which would be the best route to follow when the earth starts to shake. The wet grass ahead of you bulges upwards, forming a mound – and the side of the mound contorts into a face! An impossibly wide mouth opens and howls with deafening force. The very earth is screaming, and its cries are accompanied by the most violent quake yet. You will have to try very hard not to lose your footing as you run across the slippery grass. *Test your Skill*. If you succeed, turn to **88**. If you fail, turn to **378**.

248

Leaving the casket where it lies, you are about to depart when you hear the sound of horses' hoofs. Could it be? Your heart pounds as you move over to the door. It is!

The Shadow Warriors are storming across the fields. Will you stay inside the cave in the hope that they'll ride past (turn to **111**), or make a run for it, lest they trap you here (turn to **37**)?

249

You stand little chance of beating your omnipotent foe – but you must do your best, for the sake of the world. Each time you lose an Attack Round of combat, any STAMINA points you lose must be *added* to Voivod's current total – he thrives on your death!

VOIVOD   SKILL 10   STAMINA 10

If you win, turn to **303**.

250

Using almost all your remaining reserves of energy, you dive to one side, just as the Slygore drops down on the stone where, moments earlier, you lay. Pressed hard against the curved sewer-wall and a mere metre away from the creature, you ignore the pain and stagger to your feet. But your fading vision is filled with images of the Slygore rising. You must flee. *Test your Luck*. If you are Lucky, turn to **180**; if you are Unlucky, turn to **365**.

251

'Very persuasive,' you say mockingly, 'but your new regime will be one of death. Take a look at yourself. By your own admission, you should be mere ashes in a grave – but no: the earth has spat you out. And although you cling desperately to this "life", it torments you. Your body is stretched beyond its limits. Your Wamphyri existence is a mockery of life.'

With each passing word, Urtha grows more and more enraged until – 'Enough!' she cries. 'I will show you what it is to be immortal. Name your challenge.' Will you:

Put her to the stake?	Turn to 201
Tell her to free the Haggwort?	Turn to 331
Have her submit to the time-honoured method of destroying Undead: decapitation?	Turn to 161

252

Ennian fights like a crazed animal, and his blood, which is green, is enough to distract you from the business in hand. But you must finish the Burgomeister before his reinforcements arrive.

ENNIAN   SKILL 9   STAMINA 7

If you defeat him in five rounds or fewer, turn to 84. But if Ennian is alive after five Attack Rounds, turn to 107.

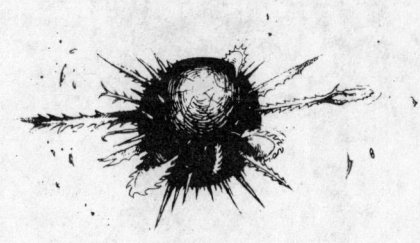

253

Descending a long, wide staircase, you come to a crossroads. Will you go:

North?	Turn to 266
South?	Turn to 291
East?	Turn to 232
West?	Turn to 144

254

You have chosen wrongly. A mystic force shoots painfully up your arm and stuns you (deduct 2 points from your STAMINA). The force also alerts those who dwell within the temple. Three sickle-wielding Geomancers arrive and drag you into the temple's anteroom, beyond which no outsider may go. They hold you there until their master, the Arch-druid, appears. Like them, he is clad in robes of shimmering white, but is more aged and splendid. He declares through his massive silver beard, 'Though your coming has been foretold, you have trespassed on forbidden lawns. You must accept the Challenge of the wise Earth-mother. The reward is freedom, the penalty is death.' Before you know it, the three Geomancers force you to your knees and interlock their sickle blades to form a razor-sharp triangle around your neck. The aged master continues, 'I call up the Challenge of the Earth-mother. On your head be understanding. Equal length between, yet unequal in length. What are we, the equinox or the solstice?' If you think the answer to his conundrum is 'the equinox', turn to **380**; if you think the correct answer is 'the solstice', turn to **332**.

255

As all the performers are tied up at the campfire meeting, now seems like a good time to investigate the circus. Will you:

Search the clown's wagon?	Turn to **333**
Search the big top?	Turn to **179**
Search the Hall of Dreams wagon?	Turn to **387**
Try and hear what's being said around the campfire?	Turn to **302**
Rush all nine of them in a surprise attack?	Turn to **45**

256

Realizing that there is nothing to be gained by lying, you come clean and tell the Orcs something of your mission. 'Hah! See!' spits Uggamonggo at his shaman. 'Spy, my gut! It's a mercenree, a good solid fighter like wot we are. Free the mercenree!' The Orcs release you, while the shaman hobbles off in disgrace, having lost another round in the continuing power struggle with her own leader. Uggamonggo suddenly takes 5 Gold Pieces out of a pouch hanging at his waist and gives them to you. 'We cud do wiv someone like yoo in our battle. This iz yer payment, mercenree.' You are just putting the gold away – as refusing the offer would mean certain death – when a volley of arrow-fire comes flying through the air. Uggamonggo shouts, 'It's a surprise attack!' Indeed, you see the Orcs of the Big Boulder charging the encampment. Will you use the confusion to try and slip away (turn to **218**), or honour your – albeit forced – contract and stand your ground alongside Uggamonggo (turn to **42**)?

257

Only the foolhardy peer into an Orb of Mind-snaring. You have lost your will to the crystal, where it will stay until Hegmar returns to free it ... Unfortunately the magician is dead, so you will be lost in this limbo for all eternity.

258

The door refuses to open, but your rattling of the handle has alerted someone on the other side. The hissing noise stops abruptly and a weary, aged voice calls out, 'Who's there? If you've come to torment me again, begone. Is it not enough to keep me locked up all these years? If you really mean to free me, find the Copper Key. And a word of advice: go wherever you think she is.' You raise your voice, trying to press the inmate for more information, but your questions are met with silence. There's nothing left for you to do but go back to the junction. There, will you now go straight on (turn to **296**), to the right (turn to **139**), or to the left, out of the caves, (turn to **80**)?

259

This Shadow Warrior is a master swordsman, wielding with consummate ease a pair of razor-edged broadswords, one in each hand. Each time you lose an Attack Round against this foe, you must deduct 4 points from your STAMINA instead of the usual 2. Armour or *Testing your Luck* may not be used to reduce this damage.

Third SHADOW WARRIOR   SKILL 9   STAMINA 9

If you defeat the Warrior, turn to **335**.

260

The Chameleon Cloak works like a dream: the Haggwort does not see you as you slip past it and press on along the road. Further on, you remove the cloak and study your surroundings. The moors look too dangerous, so you decide to keep to the road. Will you now go to the town (turn to **367**) or towards the strange tower (turn to **142**)?

261

There is a loud twanging sound as the ropes snap. The bridge swings down into the chasm, and the Dark Elves fall, screaming, to their doom. Your joy fades, however, when you hear more cultists arriving, on *your* side of the chasm! Quickly, will you go to the left (turn to **32**) or to the right (turn to **278**)?

262

After a few promising turns, the alley comes to a dead end. The only way out is back towards the street; but even now you can see a city guard coming towards you from that direction. You are bracing yourself for combat when you hear a metallic clang; you have stepped on a manhole cover. Will you lift the cover and descend into the city sewers (turn to **375**), or stand your ground and face the solitary city guard (turn to **46**)?

263

Your heroic action stops the tolling of the Iron Bell – the dead shall not walk just yet. But as long as Voivod exists, the evils will continue to multiply; it is the task of such objects as the Iron Bell to summon and guide these evils; turn to **73**.

264

You have chosen correctly: the moon reflects the light of the sun and it obscures the sun in an eclipse; the sun cannot eclipse the moon and its light is its own. As the gates open before you, however, you cannot help but sense that you have lost something in your success. Hurriedly you make your way round to the back of the temple and soon you come to another gate, leading out of the grounds. You open it and enter a narrow street. Will you now go to the left (turn to **301**) or to the right (turn to **118**)?

265

You have had enough of the Orc's insults, and you decide to teach him a lesson – but all the veterans get up and stand in your way; even the landlord hovering in the background, ready to hit you from behind. The assassin just laughs, 'Typicull Gallantree scum.' Will you press on with your attack (turn to **132**), back down and ask the men why they're spending their time with such a foul creature (turn to **287**), or turn your back on them and buy yourself a drink (turn to **3**)?

266

An eldritch fire courses through your veins and destroys you in a blaze of agony ... or so it seems, for your body lies sleeping at the foot of the wide staircase. You came down the steps just the once, before being put to sleep by the *true* Guardian of the Gate. Your repeated

descent, since then, has all been part of a never-ending nightmare from which you shall never escape.

267

Though you are fit to drop with tiredness, you persist in your journey southwards. It is mid-afternoon when you first spy an oddly shaped hill to the east. As you look at the hill, you start to feel dizzy. If you have a Green Leaf Brooch, turn to 90. If you do not, turn to 399.

268

Just as you thought – there is more Mandrake magic at work here! Looking into the mirror, you can see that the tent is plastered with bizarre messages, which all add up to some form of mind control! Though your eyes don't see the words, your mind does – and the clash is what is causing your headache. This is magic at its most loathsome! If you want to, you may use the lanterns hanging on the main pole to set fire to the tent and all its evil messages (turn to 239). Otherwise, there is nothing more you can do here; return to 255 and choose an option you have not picked before.

269

'So, yoo don't wanna tell uzz, eh?' Uggamonggo nods and the grinning Orc torturer turns the handle of the stretch rack. The frame extends, pulling on your bones, and rows of little spikes dig into your flesh (deduct 2 points from your STAMINA). Uggamonggo shouts, 'Now, are yoo gonna talk (turn to 198), or am I gonna have ta keep dis up (turn to 146)?'

270

The tattooist's expression betrays a mixture of puzzlement and vexation. 'Well, what are you doing in here, then?' he asks angrily. Will you tell him that you are hiding from Woad's men (turn to **396**) or that you are a city hygiene inspector who has come to check on the cleanliness of his tattoo parlour (turn to **236**)?

271

The more closely you inspect the encampment, the more horrifying the situation becomes. Guignol told you that he was alone: he lied. Searching through the tents, you find the belongings of seven other people – his colleagues; and then you find their bodies, tossed into a hastily dug trench. Guignol must have murdered each and every one of them. Surely, this could not have been the result of an academic dispute, however heated! If you wish, you may take a sword that you find in one of the tents. Then roll four dice and add together the numbers rolled. If the total is equal to or lower than your current STAMINA score, you may either leave the dig (turn to **282**) or try to destroy the skeleton (turn to **294**). But if the total is higher than your current STAMINA score, turn to **385**.

272

You have wasted much precious time in Royal Lendle, but the South Gate is in sight at last. It is a massive, counterbalanced, two-door structure made of heavily reinforced steel, and is set in the awesome city wall which is so thick as to have tunnels and defensive posts built into it. There is not much traffic passing through the exit and the gate wardens there are concerned with searching a trader's caravan, so no one notices when you are pulled into a derelict shack by a figure, clad head to foot in black robes. Though he is veiled, you recognize the swarthy face of a Man-Orc. He wields an evil-looking blade with manic ferocity, and hisses with hatred: 'Die, fool. Neither you nor your peasant friends shall reach Karnstein alive. My masters' will be done!' Then he is upon you.

MAN-ORC ASSASSIN   SKILL 8   STAMINA 8

If you win without losing any STAMINA points, turn to 40; if you win but *have* been wounded, turn to 4.

273

The corridor is narrow and dark, so dark that it is only luck that stops you from putting a foot out over a bottomless chasm. The chasm is too wide to jump across. If you have a rope and grapple, turn to 355. If you haven't, turn to 202.

274

The struggle over, you search the body of your fallen adversary and find 2 Gold Pieces and Provisions enough for 1 meal. Now you have time either to drink from the Wizard's Well (turn to **58**), continue northwards in search of the 'dead' hermit (turn to **349**), or leave the area altogether and head back south (turn to **44**).

275

You bowl the glowing crystal along the ground so that it comes to a stop right in the middle of the Haggwort – but they have no minds of their own to lose! One of the Haggwort picks up the sphere and tosses it aside into the quicksand (cross it off your *Adventure Sheet*). Now will you:

Attack the Haggwort in the hope of destroying their device?	Turn to **379**
Wait to see what their device does next?	Turn to **153**
Go and find the witch?	Turn to **142**
Leave the town while you still can?	Turn to **25**

276

You wet the petrified lips of the young scholar with the antidote, and in less than a minute he is moving again. 'Thank the gods!' he cries. Then he looks nervously around the room and flees into the darkness fearing another meeting with the Gorgon. But his shouted exclamation has already drawn unwanted attention. There's a scuffling in the shadows behind the six remaining statues. If you have a mirror, turn to **322**; if not, *Test your Luck*. If you are Lucky, turn to **21**. But if you are Unlucky, turn to **34**.

277

Just as you pass through the door, a full chamber pot falls from above, narrowly missing you, and lands with a thud, spilling its stinking contents all over the carpet. You have entered a cosy little room, occupied by a nice old granny who has just risen to her feet and started to scream, 'Burglars! Thieves! Help, help!' The city guards will be only too quick to hear her cries. You may take one of two exits from the room: a closed door leading to the rear of the building (turn to **328**), or a narrow flight of stairs, which goes up to the first floor (turn to **292**).

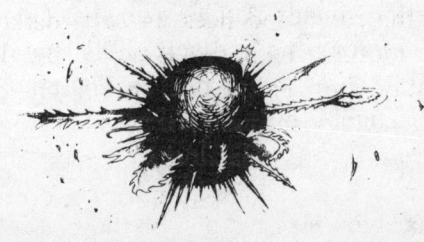

278

Entering a dark passageway, you run round a corner, then along a seemingly interminable corridor. At first you think that your eyes are playing tricks on you, but no. There *is* daylight at the end of the tunnel! However, a Dark Elf cultist stands guard.

DARK ELF CULTIST   SKILL 7   STAMINA 10

If you win, turn to **316**.

279

One of the Warriors thrusts a sharp blade into your leg while carefully watching your reaction. Despite the agony caused by the wounding, you don't even bat an eyelid. Deduct 2 points from your STAMINA. It is with unbelievable relief that you see the Warriors turn and head back to the south, out of the pass. Turn to **102**.

280

Gritting your teeth, you raise your weapon and let it fall. You stumble backwards, clutching your wrist in agony. Deduct 4 points from your STAMINA and 1 point from both your *Initial* SKILL score and your current SKILL score. Tearing a strip of cloth from your tunic, you manage to stanch the wound. Wait, what's that skittering sound? You look down on the floor and see your severed hand, moving on its fingertips, like a big spider! It tenses so that it can spring up at you. You will have to fight it off.

POSSESSED HAND   SKILL 5   STAMINA 2

If you win, you stagger out of the Hall of Dreams.

Return to 255 and choose an option you have not picked before.

281

You tug on the fine metal cord and hear a feeble tinkling sound within. A minute or so passes before the door opens. A young woman, holding a candle, silently ushers you in. Having barred the door behind you, she leads you up a long spiral staircase and into a cosy study. Plush furniture, bookcases and expensive ornaments are arranged round a comforting log fire. The lady asks you to sit down, then fetches you a goblet of fine wine and a tray of roasted meats and vegetables. If you are keen to tackle this hearty repast, turn to 235. If you would rather leave it until you know a little more about your host, turn to 99.

282

At last – Karnstein! Nestling beneath the mountains of the Witchtooth Line, the once pleasant village has been razed to the ground. Tears fill your eyes as you walk through streets that are littered with corpses. You must avenge the villagers, you must stop ... Voivod! Have

the Shadow Warriors already found the ancient Warlord? Despairing, you fall to your knees and beg the people of Karnstein for forgiveness.

'Not too late,' gasps a voice. A man, close to death, lies nearby. 'Voivod ... gone ... to raise army ... from the dead ... take thisssss ...' then he is dead. A piece of paper flaps in his hand. You take it and see that it is a map of the local area. You must use it in some way to find Voivod – note this paragraph number on your *Adventure Sheet*, as you will have to refer to the map again later.

Now think back over your adventure. If you have *either* visited the Burning Balrog Tavern *or* searched for the Hermit, turn to **388**. If you have visited *both* these places, turn to **229**. If you have been to *neither*, or have been to either or both of them but have also travelled with the Circus of Dreams, or have been a captive of the Orcs of the Black Scorpion, turn to **215**.

283

The corridor opens out into a vast natural cavern, which is rent in half by a bottomless chasm. A slender rope-bridge offers the only way across. Your pursuers are more used to these caves than you are, and four of them have almost caught up with you. If you have any Calthrops, you may throw a set down before you cross the bridge. If you do so, cross the Calthrops off your *Adventure Sheet* and roll one die. The number rolled gives you the number of cultists you shake off. Those you manage to lose in this way should come from the bottom of the list, below. You must fight any who continue the chase, one after the other.

	SKILL	STAMINA
First CULTIST	7	7
Second CULTIST	8	5
Third CULTIST	6	6
Fourth CULTIST	9	7

If you win – or if you lose them all – turn to **343**.

284

Deciding to forgo any formalities, you rap the woman's hand. She yelps and lets go of her husband, who runs away, terrified. Perplexed, you ask the woman what's wrong. She answers by making claws of her hands and attacking you.

SMILING WOMAN   SKILL 7   STAMINA 9

If you win, turn to **376**.

285

Possessed by a sudden rage, you charge the Haggwort which are bent over Wulf's helpless form, and vent your fury. Haggwort head after Haggwort head explodes (restore 1 LUCK point for your bravery). Then the threat passes. Wulf clasps your forearm and forces a grim smile. 'Just like old times, eh?'

Beyond the barricade, the six Haggwort plunge their device into the earth, where it starts to emit a low hum ... a hum which builds up into a deafening earthquake! The ground splits beneath your feet, the barricade falls apart, and bricks start to fall from nearby houses. The townsfolk flee in a blind panic, the Haggwort close behind them. If things go on as they are, the whole town could be shaken apart. Will you:

Attack the six Haggwort so that you can disable their device?	Turn to 379
Wait and see what happens?	Turn to 153
Roll an Orb of Mind-snaring – if you have one – into the middle of the six?	Turn to 275
Go and deal with the witch?	Turn to 142
Flee Hustings altogether?	Turn to 25

286

Suddenly, a grimy hand reaches out and yanks you into an alley. There, you find yourself standing face to face with Bartolph the gambler and two thugs, one of whom blocks your way back to the street. The gambler sports a number of fresh cuts and bruises, no doubt given to him by the patrons of the First Step. 'Care for more sport?' he sneers. You will have to fight all your assailants at the same time.

	SKILL	STAMINA
BARTOLPH	6	7
First THUG	7	6
Second THUG	5	7

If you win, you may either search the bodies of your enemies (turn to 243), leave them, run out of the alley and up the street before any guards, drawn by the noise of the fight, arrive (turn to 360), or rush further on down the alley, in the hope of finding a hiding place (turn to 262).

287

Confused, you ask, 'What are three reputable warriors like yourselves doing, listening to a villainous Man-Orc assassin?'

Your question meets with instant outrage. The fighter in the wide-brimmed hat strides forward and shouts, 'Are you calling my mate an Orc? That's no way to address a Femphreyan monk.'

Monk? What is he on about? Either the veterans have been drugged, or the assassin is using some sort of magical disguise. The Man-Orc sniggers and says, 'Catch.' He lobs towards you the black sphere he's been tossing in his hand. If you catch the sphere, turn to **98**. If you let it fall, turn to **326**.

288

The leader, Uggamonggo, orders two of his men to seize you. They refuse. You groan, then watch as a scrap breaks out. Two cracked skulls later, the leader has reasserted his authority. He tells two more of his Orcs to seize you. There is a tense moment and a shared intake of breath ... until the Orcs step forward, one of them sniggering wheezily. They strip you of both your armour and your weapon (if you have either, cross it off your *Adventure Sheet*), then tie you by the wrists and ankles to a pole, which they carry over their shoulders. Uggamonggo grunts, 'Right, we're off to bash the Orcs ov the Big Boulder ta prove who's the boss tribe in this place. Dunna fret, I'll keep yoo safe, 'cuz I wanna pick yer brain about pol-it-i-kul matterz.' Then the Orcs move out. They travel incredibly fast, stopping for nothing. Strange as it may seem, they are doing you a favour, taking you over the mountains in half the time it would have taken you alone. Sundown comes and the Orcs stop to make camp. Uggamonggo severs your bonds and offers you one of two chores: you can either clean their boots (turn to **93**) or help make the evening meal (turn to **81**).

289

Sadly, the well-dressed woman is the most abused of the day's ranters, and she has already added a few mouldy fruit to her personal jewellery. Nevertheless she labours on, and you discover that her cause is one that is quite close to your own heart: 'Nobody wants these meddling magicians who claim to be so important for the defence of the world. They are too powerful. They already possess enough force to destroy every living creature on Titan five times over. Does anybody ask *us* whether or not *we* want this kind of protection? *No!* It's only a matter of time before Titan is destroyed, either by war or by accident. Common people must unite to bring an end to this insanity. Abolish all High Magicks. Now!'

Just then, a whooshing sound is heard in the air, and everyone looks up to see a vermilion fireball arcing down through the sky towards the woman. Since you yourself are near her, you may shield the woman by throwing yourself into the path of the fireball. Will you do this (turn to **341**), or do you stand well back (turn to **6**)?

290

You must fight the horrible Crombane all at the same time. Their mouths spit a mild acid which ruins armour. If you are wearing armour and are hit by a Crombane in an Attack Round, you must deduct 2 hits from the armour's total, instead of the normal 1. If you are not wearing any armour, the acid does not affect you.

	SKILL	STAMINA
First CROMBANE	6	6
Second CROMBANE	7	6
Third CROMBANE	6	5
Fourth CROMBANE	5	7

If you win, you may either head for the copse (turn to **63**), run directly to the south, towards Hustings (turn to **135**), or go back northwestwards, to the safety of the road (turn to **160**).

291

Descending a long, wide staircase, you come to a crossroads. Will you go:

North?	Turn to **169**
South?	Turn to **114**
East?	Turn to **304**
West?	Turn to **266**

292

The creaking wooden steps end in a low, musty bedroom, dimly lit by the light coming from a single window. There are no other doors leading out of the room, so you make for the window. After an easy climb, you find yourself standing on the flat roof of the house, two storeys high, with a commanding view of the area. The streets are crawling with Quinsberry's lackeys. Any thoughts of escape by running from rooftop to rooftop are shattered when you see that all the neighbouring buildings are set at a distance from the one you are on. However, an alley runs down one side of the house, and in this alley stands an unattended horse. Behind you, a huffing and puffing guard has just managed to follow you up on to the roof. You will either have to fight this guard (turn to **392**) or do something you've always dreamed of: jump down on to the horse's back and ride off into the distance (turn to **100**).

293

Just inside the doorway stands a jack-in-the-box – only this 'jack' is a boxing glove on the end of a spring. You manage to duck just in time, and the glove punches a few splinters out of the door-frame. Stepping round the box, you search the wagon. Only two items seem worthy of further investigation. Which will you look at first: the safe (turn to **59**) or a large book that is lying on the clown's desk (turn to **325**)?

294

You cannot help but think that this monstrous-looking skeleton is in some way responsible for the macabre events which have overtaken the site. As you climb the flimsy wooden scaffold that has been erected over the thing, you feel instinctively drawn to its immense skull. You lift a pick-axe, ready to smash the cranium into tiny pieces. Roll four dice and add the numbers together.

If the total of the four dice is equal to or less than your current STAMINA score, turn to **329**. If the total is higher than your current STAMINA score, turn to **385**.

295

The long and winding staircase brings you to the cult's innermost sanctum: the secret chamber where the cruel and misguided Dark Elves keep their 'god' a prisoner! Across the room is another staircase, leading upwards this time. But before this exit is a treasure mound, and on this mound lies something totally beyond the range of your experience. It looks like a cross between a cobra, a goat and a man, and it has six sword-wielding arms. Fortunately the creature is asleep at the moment, and it is bound to the wall by a strand of magic. You are sneaking across to the other staircase when you catch sight of a magic ring lying on the floor. You are about to pick it up when the creature's arms start waving their swords at you. The thing is waking up! If you have some manacles, you can use them to bind the creature while you either attack it or make good your escape. If you wish to bind two of its arms together, turn to **167**. If you wish to bind its ankles together, turn to **337**. But if you have no manacles, turn to **307**.

296

The corridor you take looks fairly wide and promising, but it takes just one noise to bring you to a dead halt. From round the corner, just ahead of you, comes the hissing of a dozen snakes. If you wish to continue round this corner, turn to **352**. Otherwise, you must go back to the junction and go either to the left (turn to

139), to the right, which will take you out of the caves (turn to **80**), or straight ahead (turn to **217**).

297

In the darkness you don't even see the dozens of hands that reach out and seize you. You are powerless to resist, as the cultists drag you to their sacrificial altar!

298

The conflict at the barricade is furious: though the townsfolk are fighting a losing battle, they make the Haggwort fight every step of the way. Seeing that the townsfolk don't seem to know of the Haggwort's weakness, you cry out, 'Strike for their heads!' Three Haggwort heads explode in quick succession.

'Tonight is their greatest assault yet,' gasps Wulf, who once more fights at your side.

Quick! A Haggwort has broken through the barricade and is coming for you.

| HAGGWORT | SKILL 9 | STAMINA 5 |

If you win, turn to **213**.

299

Taking Quinsberry aside for a moment, you suggest that it might be more beneficial for him, personally, if you can come to some sort of an agreement between you. Sure enough the dry-faced official proves to be amenable to your bribe. Making no attempt to quieten his voice, he declares, 'These are the terms: you give me all the gold that you do have, together with any equipment — save for your weapon which, I appreciate, is the main tool of your trade. In exchange, I will give you another week, seven more days in which to find the money or make yourself scarce. Of course, if you opt for the latter action, I shall have no choice but to declare you an outlaw. These terms are not open to negotiation.' Will you accept this rough deal (turn to **233**), decline and surrender to Gallantarian law (turn to **199**), or turn and flee (turn to **338**)?

300

Lungs almost bursting, you flee from the mad town — and are flung to the ground by a massive explosion! Gornt has become an inferno. Huge clouds of smoke billow up into the air, bringing with them the strong smell of explosive powder. Is this the work of the Mandrakes, or an act of brave suicide? Rubble lands all around you as you slowly get to your feet and a singed piece of paper floats gently down before you. It is a brightly coloured leaflet promoting the 'Circus of Dreams'. You look at the dates on the paper. The circus was due to be in Gornt for seven days, and was leaving this very morning! Throwing the hand-out aside, you take up the Main Trade Route once more.

Though weary, you walk through the night, and it is sunrise when you come to a fork in the road. Will you stay on the Main Trade Route (turn to **267**) or head south-west (turn to **227**)?

301

Royal Lendle's East Gate towers before you. Two enormous, counterbalanced doors, constructed from heavily reinforced steel, are set into an awesome city wall which is so thick that it has defensive posts and tunnels built into it. You are shocked to discover Quinsberry Woad, waiting there for you with five of his men. If you either have a Scroll of Civic Pardon or are hiding in a rubbish cart, you may pass through the gate unhindered (turn to **145**). Otherwise, you will have to try and rush through; this will be made easier if you can create a diversion.

Test your Luck, subtracting 1 from the roll for each set of Fire-crackers which you choose to throw (always assuming you have any), to distract the guards (don't forget to cross them off your *Adventure Sheet*). If you are Lucky, your bid for freedom succeeds (turn to **145**). If you are Unlucky, you are captured by the guards (turn to **208**).

302

Though it is dark, the campfire is bright – and the circus performers are sitting in a circle, which means that at least one of them may catch sight of you, whichever way you approach. But approach you must, for they are speaking in whispers. *Test your Luck*. If you are Lucky, turn to **228**; if you are Unlucky, turn to **315**.

303

Guided by a misplaced and hopeless sense of valour,

you defy the odds and beat the armoured Warlord into the ground. But Voivod is death, and death cannot be killed. Frantic and panic-stricken, you look up to see the shambling Undead marching towards you, their weapons raised in an ever-tightening noose of death. At journey's end comes horror. True horror. You look all about you and scream!

304

Descending a long, wide staircase, you come to a crossroads. Will you go:

North?	Turn to **172**
South?	Turn to **187**
East?	Turn to **266**
West?	Turn to **144**

305

Urtha laughs at your feeble efforts: 'A predictably mortal thing to do.' Then she commands the Haggwort to restrain you. 'We'll have no more of your pathetic tricks,' she snarls. The Haggwort hold you in a grip of iron and the Wamphyr drifts towards you. A thunderclap booms as Urtha bares her rotted fangs. When next you rise from the chair, it will be as a vampiric servant of Urtha, Wamphyri Queen of the Twilight Realm.

306

Beneath the scrutiny of five sets of undying eyes, you try not to prevent even a muscle twitching. *Test your Luck*. If you are Lucky, turn to **279**; if you are Unlucky, turn to **346**.

307

The creature blinks once, twice, then it is upon you. Its mighty hoofs shake the very stone beneath your feet as it powers towards you. Each Attack Round, all six of its arms attack you at the same time (each with a SKILL score of 8), but you may strike back against only one of them, as if fighting six separate opponents. If you win against any of its other arms, your blows have no effect, serving only as parries. You will be fortunate to survive this encounter with one of the ancient Kalundai.

KALUNDAI   SKILL 8   STAMINA 20

If you win, turn to **320**.

308

Though your footsteps echo between the cavern walls, the atmosphere of the place hangs heavy, with an eerie silence. Ahead, the corridor opens out into a large and decorous chamber in which stand seven statues; you recognize them as the victims of a Gorgon's stare. Right in front of you, a vial of antidote rests on a stone column. Unfortunately, there is enough antidote to restore only one of the victims. You look at the statues; all of them deserve freedom, but not all of them can help *you*. And, right now, it isn't a sword arm you need, it's knowledge – a precious commodity these days. You narrow your choice down to two scholarly-looking figures. Look at the picture opposite and make your choice. Will you give the antidote to the old man (turn to **237**) or to the young man (turn to **276**)?

309

Your efforts come to nothing, for, though the rope is damaged, it is strong enough to hold up the bridge. One of the cultists attacks you with a sacrificial dagger, while others ready their bows. You must defeat your foe before it is too late.

DARK ELF CULTIST   SKILL 7   STAMINA 8

If you win, you may either return to cutting the ropes (turn to **261**) or leave them alone and flee (turn to **327**)?

310

Making your appeal to the veterans, you say, 'For pity's sake, my friends, our nations are at peace. I mean you no ill-will. But what of your friend? Are his hateful insults the words of a true monk?' You point at the Orc. 'Tell me, Orc, which gods do you worship?'

In reply, the Orc merely belches and grunts, 'None o' yer bizness, yer fat barrel of hogswill!' And that's all it takes to convince the veterans that you are wrong. There has to be magic at work here, there has to ... Hanging round the Orc's neck is an amulet covered in runes; this is what is responsible for both the Orc's disguise and his persuasive abilities. If you have a vial of Sleeping Draught, turn to **195**. If you do not, you will have to try and snatch the amulet from round his neck. *Test your Skill*. If you succeed, turn to **120**; but if you fail, turn to **132**.

311

Roll one die to see which of the Shadow Warriors has ambushed you. When, after defeating the Warrior, you are told to continue your adventure, you may return to the tower (turn to **141**), search further in the town (turn to **340**) or take the southbound road out of Cumbleside (turn to **75**). If you roll:

1	Turn to 8
2	Turn to 394
3	Turn to 259
4	Turn to 183
5	Turn to 245
6	Roll again

312

You go over and gaze into the depths of the perfectly smooth crystal; and as you do so, it begins to glow as if lit by eldritch fires from within. Soon you find that you have no interest in anything save the seductive dazzle of the sphere. Fortunately a remote part of your mind realizes what is happening and urges you to resist. A superhuman effort of will is called for to free you from the crystal's lure. *Test your Luck*. If you are Lucky, turn to **10**; if you are Unlucky, turn to **257**.

313

Soon you have the rope tied firmly round your body and are climbing over the lip of the dark hole. Smegg plays out more and more rope, as you go down and down, deeper into the shaft. 'Now you know why Smeggies pit!' snarls Smegg up above. You look up, worried, but can only spin helplessly as Smegg uses his spider-jaw blade to sever the rope. You fall, screaming, to your doom. Smegg will climb down later and take his pickings ...

314

No sooner does Hammicus unbar the door than it is flung wide open by the foul, undead corpse of his son! The creature strides in and grabs Hammicus by the throat. The hermit, unable to defend himself, falls to his knees, choking. You rush to help him, but the undead creature ignores your strongest blows as, single-mindedly, it concentrates on strangling the life out of the hermit.

Soon it is all over. Hammicus lies dead, and his son falls on top of him, lifeless once more. The moment Hammicus opened the door, there was nothing you could have done to save him. It is with a heavy heart that you bury both the hermit and his son in the woodland near by, then make your way back south. Tragedy seems to be dogging your every move. Deduct 1 point from your LUCK and turn to **44**.

315

You hear the clown shout, 'We have a spy in our midst. It is the mercenary. Quick! Catch the spy at once!' Obeying their leader's command, the circus folk come after you. Realizing that the game is up and that you cannot hope to defeat them all without having surprise on your side, you make a run for it. But it does look as if you're not going to be swift enough. If you have a set of Calthrops, turn to **104**. If you don't, turn to **91**.

316

Glad to be free of the cultists, you make for the bright light of the open arch. Because you have spent almost a day skulking around in dark corridors, the sun blinds your eyes, but you race on. The Dark Elves, however, stop dead in their tracks. After countless years of living in the catacombs, they have come to fear the sun. They heap curses on you as you make good your escape. And when you open your eyes properly, you are amazed to find yourself on a low hilltop, overlooking Karnstein! You have come through the Witchtooth Line and lived to tell the tale. Turn to **282**.

317

You hurl the Fire-cracker down on to the stone floor. In the confining darkness of the sewer, the flash is all the more blinding, the explosion all the more deafening. The Slygore moans with fear and drops into the water, splashing its sewage all over you. Ears ringing and half-blind, you flee before the creature can recover its unearthly composure. Eventually you find a ladder leading back up to the surface. You scramble out of the sewers and are pleased to see that Quinsberry's men have apparently given up the chase.

If you still want to visit the east side of the market, turn to **82**; if you want to visit the west side, turn to **66**. You may not return to an area you have already visited. When you have finished any excursions, you must leave the city. Do not follow the instructions given on the market pages; turn, instead, either to **272**, if you wish to leave by the city's South Gate, or to **60**, if you wish to leave by the nearer East Gate. (Note these paragraph numbers on your *Adventure Sheet*.)

318

Following a hunch, you grab the mirror and hold it up to the face of the Kauderwelsch monster. To date, it has only ever seen the Doktor and her victims, and how they have looked. Now it sees the reflection of its own unnatural ugliness – and it holds the Doktor responsible! A solitary tear rolls down the monster's face before it goes berserk. Kauderwelsch shouts, 'No! Back Conggo. Nooo!' But it is no use: the monster grabs her and they stagger about the chamber, locked in deadly combat.

Glass containers crash to the floor, racks tumble in all directions and the monster's mournful wailing fills the air. Seizing the opportunity, you hastily free yourself. Restore 1 point of LUCK for your quick thinking and turn to **87**.

319

Manacles at the ready, you sneak up on the careless guard and pounce! The Mandrake's struggles are in vain – you soon have his wrists firmly locked behind his back (cross the manacles off your *Adventure Sheet*). Then you push him down to the floor and slip out through the gate. Turn to **300**.

320

You hear shouting coming from the top of the staircase by which you entered: 'After the intruder!' The Dark Elf cultists have discovered your presence, and a dozen of them are rushing down the stairs to search for you. You quickly pick up the magic ring from the floor and make for the other staircase. You have found the Ring of Rabbam; it weakens necromantic beings such as the Shadow Warriors. Whenever you fight a Shadow Warrior in future, ignore its special combat instructions. Treat it as a normal creature with one attack per round causing normal damage, and ignore its special attack rules. Now you must go, before the cultists catch you – you will have to leave behind any manacles you used here (cross them off your *Adventure Sheet*). You run up the second staircase and along a long, dark corridor which ends in a fork. Will you go to the left (turn to **283**) or to the right (turn to **273**)?

321

Turning away from an annoying shyster who's trying to sell you a mongoose paperweight made of plaster, you find your way blocked by six men dressed in heavy armour; they are city guards. Once you see the gnarled old weasel who is leading them, you understand what all this is about: it is Quinsberry Woad, Gallantaria's chief tax collector, with his personal retinue. Woad produces a scroll from the depths of his overlarge robes and says, 'Captain, I am hereby authorized to serve you with this Bill of Taxes, which must be paid forthwith. In lieu of satisfactory fiscal settlement, I have an open warrant for your arrest.' He presents you with the scroll and continues, 'The original balance, charged at compound interest, half-yearly and at a fixed annual percentage rate for five years, comes to 568 Gold Pieces precisely. Do you have the money?'

You clearly have not got and cannot afford to pay such a vast sum; now you regret ever returning to the capital. But what will you do? You could plead poverty and let the guards arrest you (turn to **199**), try to bribe Quinsberry Woad (turn to **299**), or turn on your heels and make a run for it (turn to **338**).

322

You snatch the mirror from your pack and brandish it in the face of the Gorgon – who falls victim to her own dark forces. But even when she herself has been turned to stone, you still avoid her repulsive gaze. There is nothing more to see or do in her lair, so you hurry back to the junction. Will you now go to the left (turn to

217), to the right (turn to **296**), or straight on, out of the caves (turn to **80**)?

323

Lightning-swift reflexes and total trust in your old friend enable you to drop prone as a razor-sharp machete goes flying over your head; it just misses Villgran and embeds itself in a tree trunk. One of the Haggwort threw it at you, the same Haggwort that Wulf has just killed. Will you now rush over to the barricade (turn to **298**), go in search of the witch (turn to **142**), or leave the town (turn to **25**)?

324

You will never regret buying the wondrous cape; the Warriors race blindly past. Leaving a cloud of dust in their wake, they sweep out of Magyaar Pass and speed northwards. Turn to **102**.

325

You have found the clown's Circus Journal. You don't have time to read all of it, but, in the few minutes you do spend on the book, you learn a couple of important things: the circus was taken over by force, a year ago, by a sorcerer named Skarros; he it was who replaced the performers with plant-like creatures called Mandrakes. These Mandrakes can take on the appearance of any one person they touch: they then kill their victim so that they can adopt his or her identity. The circus is the ideal cover for the Mandrakes, as they travel from place to place, spreading their evil plague. Fortunately, the journal also mentions the Mandrakes' only weakness – fire! Suddenly you hear a noise outside. You had better get out before your presence here is discovered. Return to **255** and pick an option you have not chosen before.

326

Convinced that the sphere is not meant to be a goodwill gift, you step aside. The moment it hits the floorboards, it bursts open into a multitude of spring-loaded spikes, blades and razor-sharp edges. You dread to think what would have happened if you had actually grasped the thing! The Man-Orc, the veterans and the landlord all laugh at your 'chicken dance'. Will you now attack the Man-Orc (turn to **132**), try to expose him for what he really is (turn to **310**), or ignore them all and go to the bar (turn to **3**)?

327

You turn and run, but the Dark Elf archers are ready for you. Roll one die and deduct 1 from the total to see how many arrows hit you – deduct 2 points from your STAMINA for each arrow that hits. If you are still alive, you keep on running, pulling the arrows out of your back as you go! But the cultists continue the chase. Worse, you can hear the shouts of more cultists coming from *this* side of the chasm. Will you now go to the left (turn to **32**), or to the right (turn to **278**)?

328

Beyond the door is a cramped kitchen, where you see a large kennel housing a labrador who lies flat, with her chin flopped on the tiled floor. As you tiptoe past, she lifts her eyebrows to peer at you, cocks an ear, yawns and then goes back to sleep. You nip out through the back door and find yourself in a narrow street. Turning right would take you back towards Quinsberry, so you turn left, and laugh when you hear the labrador growl menacingly at your pursuers, whose clattering armour and loud shouts have disturbed her rest. Turn to **22**.

329

There is a tremendously loud crunch as you shatter the ages-old skull. You sense the creature's feelings of frustration, disbelief and anger as its whole frame turns rapidly into dust. In a very short time, there is nothing left of the Pan-Terric Behemoth to prove that it ever existed. Restore 1 LUCK point for your great achievement. Glancing at the tents, the tools, the remnants of Guignol's dream, you can see nothing but tragedy. You leave the camp without disturbing it and make your way back to the road to Karnstein. Turn to **282**.

330

You rush to the hermit and restrain him. The voice outside wails, 'Father, please. You must let me in. If you don't I will die!' Overcome with emotion, Hammicus finds renewed strength and breaks free of your grasp. The only way to stop him now is by the use of regrettable force.

HAMMICUS   SKILL 5   STAMINA 7

If, after one round of combat, you decide to let the hermit open the door, turn to **314**. But if you are still determined to stop him, turn to **76**.

331

Freed from Urtha's cruel domination, the Haggwort become wild and uncontrollable. They grab the tyrant and throw her on to the mystic fire – the *real* power in

Hustings; the magic inside the Haggwort heads stems from this fiery source. It was the same magic that reanimated Urtha, and it was the only thing that could have destroyed her. She perishes instantly. Events have come full circle, the corrupted earth-magic has run its course. Something clatters at your feet; it is Urtha's Iron Band. Though you have no wish to control the Haggwort, you feel compelled to pick it up (add it to your *Adventure Sheet*). You look once more at the fireplace. The eyes and the mouth have closed, and the whole thing is starting to sink back down into the marsh – taking the tower and the pinnacle with it. You hurry out of the place before it collapses altogether, and make for the southerly road out of town. You see the Haggwort wading back into the moors, returning to their resting places once more. Turn to **25**.

332

As the Geomancers remove their sickles from around your neck, the Arch-druid raises his arms and says, 'In accordance with the ancient laws of the Horned God, you have passed the test and are free to roam the power lines of Titan. We have enacted our destinies and can do nothing more. Take this.' He pins a small brooch in the shape of a green leaf on you. 'It is a token of the Earth-mother's goodwill. Times are changing and the Mother is threatened. You are the one who will help. This has been foreseen. Now go! Look for help from Titan, for only *it* has the strength to guide you on your hopeless task.' Add the Green Leaf Brooch to your *Adventure Sheet*. The Arch-druid's servants lead you to a gate at the back of the grounds. Passing through it, you come to a narrow street. Will you go to the left (turn to **301**) or to the right (turn to **118**)?

333
Making sure that no one is watching, you creep round to the back of the clown's wagon and open the door. You sneak into the dark cabin and ... *Test your Luck*. If you are Lucky, turn to **293**. If you are Unlucky, turn to **345**.

334
Sweat pours off you as you walk for hour after hour beneath the blazing sun. You are resting in a shady hollow when you hear the tramp of marching feet and the grunting of countless voices coming from over a rise. These are the tell-tale noises of a roaming Orc tribe. You crouch down, hoping to remain hidden in the hollow, but the Orcs see you and start scampering down the slopes on either side of you to cut off your way of escape. You search for an exit out of this tightening cordon and gasp with relief when you see a cave near by. Then again, you *are* in the Witchtooth Line, where caves are never simply caves. If you want to hide inside the dark cave, turn to **206**. If you would rather try to outrun the Orcs, turn to **35**. If, on the other hand, you have a Chameleon Cloak and wish to use it to try and sneak unseen through the Orc ranks, turn to **163**.

335

Though the struggle was hard, you have defeated your foe. The Shadow Warrior falls, wailing, in an untidy heap. Yet no sooner does the evil fiend hit the ground than dark vapours start to rise from its body. You stand back and watch as the foul fumes enshroud the corpse, obscuring it from sight. When they clear, the body is no longer there. Only a scorch on the earth remains. You may have beaten the Warrior, but you have not destroyed it. It will take more than the weapons of mortal man to lay such creatures to rest: it is more than likely that you will meet one another again before this tale is told. Rue the day! Now continue your adventure.

336

The sides of the pit are sheer and your numerous attempts to climb out all end in miserable failure. Hours pass before you hear a female voice whisper, 'Don't worry, I'm coming. Just a second longer.' It is with renewed hope that you look up – into the face of a Gorgon! You turn to stone beneath her cruel gaze.

337

You clamp the creature's ankles together just in time. It tries to get up but falls flat on its face. Its eyes glare with hatred and it hisses with rage as its arms scrape along the floor towards you. You step nimbly round the creature, keeping out of the reach of its swords. It is one of the ancient Kalundai. But look! The chain of the manacles is already starting to weaken. Turn to **320**.

338

You give Quinsberry a shove so that he totters back into his guards, and they all fall over in an untidy heap. The troops raise the alarm and the taxman squawks with rage; never has he been so humiliated in his entire life. Rather than restrain you, however, the bystanders just stand there, laughing loud and long at the pompous official's plight. Before the guards can regain their feet, you flee. A few metres ahead, you come to a junction. Will you go left (turn to **351**), right (turn to **384**), or straight ahead (turn to **134**)?

339

Eager to lend a hand, you rush over to the gallant warrior and introduce yourself. 'I don't believe it,' he gasps. 'Of all the people I could've hoped for in this hour of need!' It is Wulf, your old friend and fighting companion from the War of the Four Kingdoms. You return your comrade's embrace, then listen intently as he explains. 'It started a few days ago, with the coming of the witch. Her tower just rose up out of the earth. Every night since then she's been sending the Haggwort to destroy everything in their path. Everyone's too scared to face the witch. I tried once but got nowhere. But come, the Haggwort have reached the barricade.' He points out an old man. 'That's Villgran. He has armour and swords, should you need them.'

Will you go over to Villgran (turn to **97**), accompany Wulf to the barricade (turn to **298**), or go to cut the evil off at its source, the witch's tower (turn to **142**)?

340

Leaving the body of the fallen Warrior, you begin a more thorough search of the place and encounter a fair maiden. Clutching a robe tightly round herself, she whispers. 'It is not wise to dally in these parts at night. Come. The only safe place is the tower yonder.' She points towards the tower you passed earlier, then hurries away in that direction. If you wish to follow her, turn to **372**. If you would rather continue your search, turn to **23**.

341

Though meant for the woman, the fiery spell has descended upon you. From afar, a wizard has been watching the ranter's dialogue with increasing irritation and has now decided to shut her up with a simple conjuration. Unfortunately, instead of her, it is you who have been turned into a warty frog. Karnstein, Warriors and words in general quickly lose their meaning. Now where can you find some tasty flies?

342

All the wind is knocked out of you as you are sandwiched between the door and the hard rock wall (deduct 3 points from your STAMINA). If you are still alive, you enter the dark shelter. Though heavy with the stench of Orc, the cave is well nigh bare and is uninhabited at present. Black robes and a torn map of Royal Lendle lie on the floor. The only other thing of interest is a small metal casket. It is locked – but if you have a Black Key or a vial of Metal Rot you may open it (turn to **354** – and cross off Metal Rot from your *Adventure Sheet* if you use that). But if you don't have either of these things, or would rather leave the casket alone, turn to **248**.

343

You sprint across the bridge and soon reach the far side. There, you see that it is suspended by strong ropes tied to wooden posts. More fleet-footed cultists are crossing the bridge after you. If you want to try and cut the ropes so that the bridge and all the howling cultists on it fall into the chasm, turn to **246**. If you would rather keep on running, turn to **327**.

344

You nip into the gibbering wretch's hovel and let him guide you into a back room from which there is no other exit. He tells you to wait in here until he gives you the 'all clear'. You do so, and some tense minutes pass before the door is thrown open – by seven city guards! Behind them, the old rascal gleefully toys with a second Gold Piece — the things some folk will do for money! Turn to **199**.

345

Just inside the doorway stands a small box. As you walk in, the lid of the box flips open, releasing a boxing glove on the end of a spring. It flies up and punches you on the nose (deduct 1 point from your STAMINA). Kicking the thing aside, you search the wagon. Only two items draw your attention. Which of the two do you want to look at first: the safe (turn to **59**) or a large book, lying on the clown's desk (turn to **325**)?

346

Your actions are totally futile, and your corpse soon joins those of Mendokan and the others butchered in Magyaar Pass.

347

The circumstances are perfect. You grab a Fire-cracker and hurl it to the ground in front of Ennian's mob. In the total darkness of the narrow brick-lined alley, the echoing explosion is most effective. Your enemies fall back, clutching their eyes and ears, while you, having taken the trouble to close both, make good your escape. Turn to **84**.

348

You run, in order to gain speed, then jump. Hugging your knees, you roll over and over through the air and then let go, so that your legs shoot out and catch Voivod in the chest, kicking him away from the bell.

Test your Skill. If you succeed, turn to **263**; but if you fail, turn to **133**.

349

Night has fallen by the time you reach the hermit's cottage. Hammicus the hermit is a friendly old man and he wastes no time in providing you with a hot meal (restore 2 STAMINA points). As you eat, you risk total honesty and tell Hammicus all about your quest. Frowning, he goes over to consult a book at his desk, then says, 'Over two thousand years ago, there existed one Voivod, whose very name was a byword for cruelty. His power threatened life itself; but the world took shape in the form of the Earth-mother and the Horned God; together, they fought Voivod and defeated him. They were not able to kill death itself but could only imprison him in a secret place. Voivod's five lieutenants disappeared, never to be seen again – or so it seemed. For now we can understand the old nursery-rhyme. The Shadow Warriors have been seeking Voivod's prison in the hope of freeing him, so that he may embark on a new reign of terror. It is said that a book, the *Astrakkaans Numeris*, predicts Voivod's return and provides the means whereby he can be defeated. I don't know if the book truly exists, but I *do* know that Voivod is about to walk Titan again!'

Suddenly, there comes a heavy pounding on the door: three slow, booming knocks that almost shatter the wood. They are followed by a low, mournful voice. 'Father, it is I, your son. Please, let me in. It is so cold out here.'

Hearing this, Hammicus falls back and cries in sorrow and terror, 'It cannot be. My son *died* seven years ago!' But he overcomes his fears and makes for the door.

Unless you stop him, the hermit will admit his long-dead son. Will you try to stop the hermit (turn to **330**), or let him unbar the door (turn to **314**)?

350

Your joy at escaping vanishes when a shower of arrows comes flying overhead – not from the Orcs of the Black Scorpion, but towards them! The Orcs of the Big Boulder have arrived, planning to take their rivals by surprise. Luckily, none of the arrows hits you as you throw yourself to the ground. Will you offer your services to the Orcs of the Big Boulder, so that you can take your revenge on your captors (turn to **377**), or just let them get on with their own fighting and flee southwards (turn to **282**)?

351

The road you have taken leads into the beggars' quarter, a maze of narrow streets strewn with rubbish, layabouts and pickpockets. As you wind your cautious way towards its centre, you hear the shouts of your pursuers fade in the distance. However, it is certain that Quinsberry's men will not give up the chase, so you keep on running. If you are carrying a Loaded Die, turn to **286**; otherwise, turn to **360**.

352

Rounding the corner, you enter a large room which is strewn with clothes, personal belongings, caskets, jewellery and musical instruments, all from various periods of time. But there is no sign of what is causing the hissing – a sound which keeps getting louder! If you want to risk searching through all the things scattered about here, turn to **155**. If you do not, you will have to return to the junction and either go left (turn to **139**), right, which will take you out of the caves (turn to **80**), or straight ahead (turn to **217**).

353

Just as things are starting to look bad for you, Wulf and three brave townsfolk come to your aid. The five of you just finish off the remaining Haggwort, but you have no such luck with their evil device. Nothing you do can dislodge or damage the earth-shaker in any way. You can only watch as the nearby houses start to fall, shaken apart by the vibrations in the earth. 'All is lost!' cries Wulf. 'It's the witch's doing. We must take the south road and flee.' Will you do as Wulf suggests (turn to **25**), or leave him and go in search of the 'witch' (turn to **142**)?

354

Inside the casket is a weapon much favoured by assassins: it is a Murder Sphere, a small metal ball which you throw at your enemy. On impact, the ball turns itself inside out as spikes, razors, barbs and saws spring out in all directions. You may use the sphere in the first Attack Round of any one combat against any one opponent. When you throw it, roll one die to see how many of the sphere's protrusions hit your foe. Then roll another die for each wound inflicted, to see how many STAMINA points your foe must deduct. If your foe is still alive, you must then fight as normal.

You are just putting the sphere in your pack when you hear a noise that you have come to dread: the pounding of horses' hoofs. Rushing to the open doorway, you see the Shadow Warriors tearing across the open country. If you want to stay where you are and hide in the cave, turn to **111**. If you would rather make a run for it, before you find yourself trapped in this small place, turn to **37**.

355

You throw the hook so that it catches among the stalactites hanging down from the roof of the cave, you tug on the rope, then swing! Even you are amazed when you reach the far side of the chasm without mishap. But you will have to leave the rope behind you, as the hook is caught. On the other side of the chasm the thwarted cultists catch sight of you and shout their hatred. And you can hear more cultists, somewhere on *your* side of the chasm. Will you now go to the left (turn to **32**) or to the right (turn to **278**)?

356

Realizing the futility of combat against the Slygore, you stagger away in a bid to escape. *Test your Luck*. If you are Lucky, turn to **180**; but if you are Unlucky, turn to **154**.

357

With its strong limbs and tough coating of bark, the Mahogadon is a daunting opponent. If you wish, you may try to weaken your foe by burning it. Cross off a skin of oil from your *Adventure Sheet*, and then *Test your Skill*. If you succeed, you burn and weaken the creature. If you fail, the creature's unyielding grip forces you to drop the oil on the ground, wasting it. Whatever the outcome, you must now fight the Mahogadon as normal. If you have succeeded in burning it, deduct 2 points from its SKILL score and 4 points from its STAMINA score before beginning combat.

MAHOGADON   SKILL 10   STAMINA 12

If you win, you may either continue to the south, across more open country, towards Hustings (turn to **135**) or go back to the road you left earlier (turn to **160**).

358

Drawing nearer to the circus, you see that the dozen performers are an odd mix of acrobats, tumblers, animal trainers and so on; each is busy dealing with his or her own props. One figure seems to be in charge: it is a clown, a lithe woman already dressed in her show costume, her face covered with grease-paint depicting a fixed smile that looks almost sinister. You walk over to the clown and ask her where the circus is going and if the wagons have room for an extra passenger. Her face breaks into an even wider smile as she replies, 'We are going to Shattuck. As for passage, you will have to earn your way. Are you amusing? Can you run a sideshow? Perhaps you know a trick or two?' If you have Bartolph's die, turn to **138**. If you don't, will you ask her to give you a chance to prove your worth (turn to **214**), or admit that there's nothing you can do that would be of use to the circus, and turn away, to continue your journey alone and on foot (turn to **9**)?

359

You ignore the black slop – and wisely so, as the thing is alive. It is a Slod-Kedbolm, whose skin is poisonous. Bored with waiting around, the Slod-Kedbolm slithers away. You keep your eyes on the creature, until you are distracted by silken tones: 'It is ill-mannered to refuse hospitality.' Turn to **49**.

360

You hare up the street, with six sword-waving city guards in your wake. Not far ahead, round the corner, is a magician's shop; maybe you can shake off your hunters by hiding in there. However, experience has taught you that such places are perilous, if full of possibilities. Will you enter the magician's abode (turn to **105**), or pass it by (turn to **216**)?

361

You wake up – even the Nightmare Master's attack took place in your dreams! But now your ordeal is finally over, and you feel your strength returning (restore 3 points of STAMINA). Then you hear a low, echoing voice: 'Though I murder sleep, I can never die.' It is the Nightmare Master. Beaten for now, he departs.

Climbing to your feet, you see that you are in a small, dimly lit hallway. Four doors lead out of it. One of them opens and two figures walk out: Dark Elves, clad in monastic robes. You dodge back and hide in a shadowy alcove as they walk silently across the hall and pass through one of the other doors. They are cultists, and this is their temple. If your sacrilegious presence is detected here, you will most certainly be killed. Will you go through the north door (turn to **374**), the south door, after the two Dark Elf cultists (turn to **68**), the east door (turn to **89**), or the west door (turn to **56**)?

362

'Look at his reflection,' she says. 'Korin may be scared, but she's not stupid.' You angle the mirror so that the Burgomeister is reflected in it. Nothing could have prepared you for such a shock as this: there, in the silvered pane, stands the Burgomeister, exposed as a vegetable-like humanoid. You use the mirror to look at yourself and at Korin; you both look normal. But the Burgomeister! You try looking at him again in the mirror – and the result is the same. 'He's a Mandrake,' spits the woman.

Ennian just smiles and calls over his shoulder for some help. Then he turns back to you. 'You shouldn't have done that, it was most impolite,' he sighs. 'Still, there's no reason why we can't sort out our differences peacefully. If you'll just hand over the mirror and come quietly . . .'

Behind you, Korin runs off towards the far end of the alley. Will you follow her (turn to **84**) or attack the Mandrake Burgomeister (turn to **252**)?

363

Telling the Orcs what you think they want to hear, you admit to being a spy, sent by the Court at Royal Lendle to discover enemy movements. 'Hah! See, I told yerz,' snaps the shaman triumphantly. 'A spy. The ainshunt lawz tell uzz wot ta do ta spies, don't they?' Having lost another round in his power struggle with the shaman, Uggamonggo shrugs and, with an air of something approaching sadness, draws his long knife. Your adventure ends here.

364

Once, twice, three times the low sonorous chiming of the bell rings in your ears. Then the very ground cracks open as the bodies of the fallen rise up from their unmarked graves. Their expressionless, rotted faces await command. So far, you can see only a few hundred of them scattered about the arid landscape, but soon they will all be free – all ten thousand of them! The Voivod strikes the bell again and again. Now you rush forward to stop him, but the shambling Undead obey their master and bar your way. Roll two dice to see how many of the shambling Undead strike you as you fight your way through them. For each hit, deduct 2 points from your STAMINA. Armour and *Testing your Luck* may be used to reduce the amount of damage done to you. If you survive this battering, turn to **73**.

365

No one hears the drawn-out screams as they echo round and round the sewers. The Slygore has dropped down on top of you, and it is with a strange feeling of detachment that you realize the screams are your own.

366

You have found the vital book of numbers, written by Parcleasus the numerologist. You leaf through it until you find the most important page and tear it out of the book. You can study the page now or at any time in the future by turning to **16** (note this number on your *Adventure Sheet*). Just as you close the book, a secret panel in the far wall slides open! If you have a Chameleon Cloak, turn to **127**; otherwise, turn to **150**.

367

The people of the small town are already preparing for war, collecting whatever weapons they can lay their hands on. Upturned wagons, wooden boxes and bits of fencing form a pitiful makeshift barricade between the town and the moors. Seeing that you are human, and a stout fighter to boot, the townsfolk hurry you through the blockade. But they have no time for pleasantries; they turn their attention back to the dark silhouettes stalking the moors. Inside the barricade an armoured figure rallies his people with a call to arms: 'Stand fast. We must not fall. The witch and her devilry be damned! To arms! To arms! The Haggwort are upon us!' Will you:

Use the confusion of the battle to flee southwards, out of the town?	Turn to **25**
Make yourself known to the brave warrior and offer your services?	Turn to **339**
Slip away and investigate the strange tower on the pinnacle?	Turn to **142**

368

The door is locked. If you have a Copper Key, or a vial of Metal Rot (which you may pour into the lock – cross it off your *Adventure Sheet*), turn to **112**. If you have neither, turn to **258**.

369

Whether you fall victim to an unseen trap or to a lurking creature is unimportant. You were foolish to enter such a dangerous place without something to light the way, and you have paid the ultimate price for your folly.

370

The fight is a long and hard one, but the city guards eventually regain control. Many people have been injured and some, including all the agitators, have been killed. The guard marshal tears the dead leader's black tunic open, exposing the mark of Chaos branded on his chest! Moreover the corpse is wearing a magic pendant which made all but the strongest-willed of listeners susceptible to his foul utterances. He was just one of the many servants of Evil who are being sent to upset the uneasy alliance between the four kingdoms. Satisfied, the marshal turns to you. 'It is fortunate that you were here, mercenary,' he says, 'the struggle may otherwise have gone differently. Before this disgrace occurred, I had the chance to learn something of your plight. Therefore, as a reward for your efforts here, I grant you a Scroll of Civic Pardon. From now on, you are free of your debt to the City.' Restore 1 LUCK point, and add the Scroll of Civic Pardon to your *Adventure Sheet*.

After all this commotion, you decide that you had best be on your way to meet Mendokan's party. If you want to leave the city by the South Gate, turn to **272**. If you would rather leave by the nearer East Gate, turn to **60**.

371

You reach forward to touch the disgusting object. It is warm and slippery, and it pulsates nauseatingly.

Suddenly the mesh of tubes wraps round your hand in an iron grip. Small barbs grow out of the veins and the whole mess starts crawling up your hand. The only way to stop it going any further is by cutting off your own hand at the wrist! If you have a weapon and you want to take this drastic step, turn to **280**. If you would rather wait and see what happens, or if you don't have a weapon, turn to **85**.

372

You follow the mysterious lady back towards the old tower. She opens the single, heavy door and beckons you inside. You do so ... and see stars. She has hit you hard on the back of your head with a cosh! You fall to the floor, unconscious; turn to **186**.

373

Decide how many Gold Pieces you wish to give the highwayman, then roll one die. If you roll less than or equal to the number of Gold Pieces you have chosen, the highwayman accepts your payment and lets you go unharmed (deduct the gold from your *Adventure Sheet*). In this case, you may either continue in a northerly direction in search of the hermit who, the highwayman claims, is dead (turn to **349**); if you feel you have wasted too much time here already, you may head back south (turn to **44**). If, however, you roll higher than the number of Gold Pieces you have offered, turn to **92**.

374

You open the north door and enter what must be the cult's chamber of worship. One side of the room is

taken up by a long altar, resplendent with sacred paraphernalia. Behind the altar is a huge statue of a Dark Elf with six arms, and behind the statue is an open archway, through which you can see a descending staircase. Suddenly a loud gong resounds and the room is plunged into darkness – the glow from the walls now gone. The hall door opens behind you, and you hear a rush of footsteps come into the room. If you wish to slip down the staircase, turn to **295**. If you would rather stay where you are, turn to **297**.

375

You lift the circular lid and climb down a set of rungs into the dark sewers. Though no guards follow, you hurry on, your path running alongside a stomach-turning river of sewage. Soon, however, you are hopelessly lost in the meandering underground complex and cannot find a way back up to ground level. Things get even worse when you hear an awful moan arise from the depths of the sludge. It is with a sense of despair that your worst fears are confirmed for, lifting high out of the water to tower above you, is a dread Slygore. It is said that these creatures are unwittingly created by the city's many alchemists and sorcerers who, despite public protests, are forever polluting the city sewers with the potent by-products of their esoteric experiments. Such wastes react with the effluent to form Slygore, shambling mounds of murderous filth. Will you:

Attack the creature?	Turn to **70**
Look in your pack for something which may defeat it?	Turn to **230**
Flee from it?	Turn to **356**

376
Your victory was a hard-earned one. The woman fought like an animal, and when you struck her you saw that her blood was green! There is clearly some great evil at work here. You turn to go, but just then you hear something that freezes you to the spot: a quiet, teasing laugh coming from the woman you have just slain! You quickly turn around. Her body has gone. It is only when you hear her sly laugh again that you hurry away; turn to **231**

377
A shower of stubby Orc arrows rains down on you. Your adventure ends here.

378
Running at full speed, your right heel catches in the wet grass at an angle and slips forward. You slam into the earth, the shock of the impact coursing painfully up your spine (deduct 2 points from your STAMINA). You climb back on to your feet and watch as the ever-shifting face spews four repulsive abominations out of

its cavernous green mouth. In some ways the creatures resemble giant flies, but they have human heads, and bits and pieces from a variety of other plants, animals and insects. They are Crombanc, spawn of the dying earth, and, though they are too heavy to fly, they are powerful runners. They charge towards you, yowling like demented wolves, their disgusting legs throwing up clods of sodden earth. Will you stand and fight (turn to **290**), or flee (turn to **14**)?

379

You must fight all six Haggwort at once but, because you are in a battle-rage and because you know of their weakness, you inflict STAMINA loss on each and every one you hit.

	SKILL	STAMINA
First HAGGWORT	10	1
Second HAGGWORT	9	3
Third HAGGWORT	11	2
Fourth HAGGWORT	8	1
Fifth HAGGWORT	10	4
Sixth HAGGWORT	9	2

After two rounds of combat, turn to **353**.

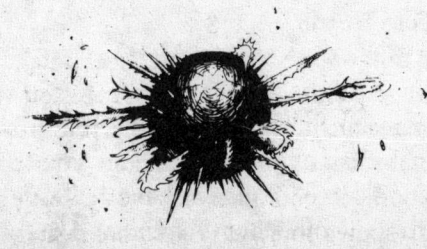

380

The three fine-honed blades swish together and close. Your adventure ends here.

381

When you hear a sharp *click* come from the floor, you don't waste any time thinking. You leap forward, just as the floor gives way beneath your feet. You have avoided falling into a deep pit. Moving on from the trap, you come to a junction. Will you go:

Left?	Turn to **296**
Right?	Turn to **217**
Straight ahead?	Turn to **139**
Back the way you came and out of the caves altogether?	Turn to **80**

382

'All is chaos and confusion,' says Jack-in-the-Green. 'Anger comes too swiftly in these troubled times and, where there is anger, death is sure to follow. Your task is to heal old wounds, to find peace in Narbury. But be warned! Violence can never be the final answer. Evil must defeat itself. Your duty is to help, not to spread further anger. When you think you have succeeded, say the word "Cerunnos" in your mind and we will see what unfolds.' Turn to **398**.

383

When you reach the bottom of the rough shaft, you discover that it is not wide enough for you to tug your grappling hook free. You will have to leave the rope behind (cross it off your *Adventure Sheet*). Looking around, you see that you have descended in the very middle of a crossroads and that the walls of the four smooth passages emit a faint glow. Will you now go:

North?	Turn to **106**
South?	Turn to **114**
East?	Turn to **122**
West?	Turn to **144**

384

Your road brings you to a small courtyard filled with fruit and vegetable stalls. The only way not barred by city guards is to take a sharp left up a narrow street. Before going round this turning, you may try and delay your pursuers by tipping over some of the stalls. If you want to do this, turn to **110**. If you would rather keep on running, turn to **78**. However, if you would like to stop and give yourself up before things get too serious, turn to **199**.

385

Though you don't really know why, you take a pick-axe and start digging. And in only a matter of hours, you have managed to cut most of the skeleton free of the sandstone. It is only then that the hands of the skeleton start moving! If you have some manacles, you may use them to bind its bony hands together. Is Guignol still alive? If so, turn to **109**. If not, turn to **185**.

386

After a few uneventful hours you reach the foothills of the mountain range. There is no way over these

treacherous peaks. Instead, your road ends at a massive, pitch-black cavemouth. This is the much-used entrance into the infamous honeycomb of tunnels which is said to permeate the entire Line. It might well be considered foolish to enter these caves at all, but it would be suicidal to enter them without a lantern. If you have a lantern and you wish to enter the cave, deduct one skin of oil from your *Adventure Sheet* and turn to **240**. If you are foolish enough to enter the cave without a lantern, turn to **369**. But if you would rather avoid the caves altogether, you will have to make your way back to the Shattuck road; turn to **334**.

387

It is with a sense of anticlimax that you discover that the Hall of Dreams is just a room full of bending, curving mirrors which ripple and distort your reflection in a supposedly humorous way. You're not laughing ... And you're still not laughing when one of the mirrors disappears, right before your very eyes, revealing a small stone chamber beyond — a chamber which cannot possibly be real since there is no way it could fit inside the wagon. You lift your hand and move it slowly through the 'mirror' frame. The room *is* real! Looking inside, you see a man-sized shape leaning against a stone slab. It is alive with all sorts of fearsome growths and a mesh of revolting veins hangs down from it to the floor, where they are wrapped round the withered carcass of a badger. The veins have sucked all the life-juices out of the poor animal. Without warning, another mesh of veins shoots out towards you, but falls short. If you have read Hegmar's Warning, turn to **204**.

If you have not, you may either touch the mesh of veins (turn to **371**), attack the foul creature (turn to **157**), or leave the place altogether. If you decide to leave, return to **255** and pick an option you have not chosen before.

388

Looking at the map, you need to know two things: the first is where you think Voivod will be right now – you will need a degree of common sense to work this out. Once you have decided where, on the map, Voivod is, you will have to turn that place-name into numbers. If you have this knowledge, set to work immediately. When you think you have found the right number, turn to it. If the entry you turn to does not make sense, you have chosen wrongly. If the entry does make sense, carry on with the adventure. Because you have taken so long to reach the village, you get only one shot at this. If you choose wrongly, or if you just don't know how to find Voivod in the first place, turn to **229**.

389

Your ploy works like a dream: dozens of people all round you scramble in a mad hunt for the few pitiful coins you have scattered among them. The city guards rush forward to quell the chaos, leaving the exits from the square unguarded. Are you tempted by the sight of the green and pleasant grounds of a small temple, bordered by a low wall (turn to **164**), or do you steal away down a narrow lane (turn to **118**)?

390

Only when you reach the 'man' do you realize that 'he' is far from human. Darkness prevents you from seeing just what the creature is, but you have no trouble hearing its swamp-gurgled snarls, or in catching the glint of the vicious blade it swings towards you!

HAGGWORT   SKILL 10   STAMINA 4

If you win, turn to **5**.

391

While at the stores, you cast an eye over the equipment for sale there. You may buy a sword for 2 Gold Pieces, or a mace for 4 Gold Pieces; the mace costs foes 3 points of STAMINA each time they are hit (4 points if you *Test your Luck* successfully, but no points if you are unsuccessful). For 5 Gold Pieces you may also buy a suit of leather armour. Though the armour is not built to last, it's incredibly tough. It can take a total of 5 hits before it becomes useless. If you are hit while wearing leather armour, you lose only 1 point of STAMINA instead of 2 (no points of STAMINA if you *Test your*

Luck successfully, but 4 points if you are unsuccessful). You must also add 1 to any *Test your Skill* rolls you make while wearing the armour. If you buy anything here, add it to your *Adventure Sheet* and deduct the gold you spend. Unfortunately, no one in the stores has heard of any 'man of numbers', so you will have to continue your search in either the taverns (turn to **209**) or the town square (turn to **27**).

392

You do not want to kill the guard – but you won't have to if you can disarm him. Being a professional, he will surrender once he loses his sword. Fight the guard as normal but, if you hit him, you do not injure him (for that reason the guard does not have a STAMINA score). Nothing happens unless your score in any Attack Round is at least 3 points higher than the guard's, in which case you disarm him and the combat ends. Note that he has no qualms about injuring you.

CITY GUARD   SKILL 8

More guards are climbing up on to the roof even as you are fighting. If you have not disarmed your foe after four rounds, you will be captured (turn to **199**). If you do win, you will have to jump down on to the horse after all (turn to **100**).

393

Moonlight paints the night-time landscape with an eerie silvery glow, illuminating your first view of Cumbleside. This town was abandoned long ago, its residents weary of having to guard themselves against the constant stream of malice which descended on them from the Witchtooth Line: Ogres, Demons, Goblin raiding-parties and worse. You are passing through the outskirts of the town when you come to a tall tower, standing alone like a needle in the darkness. A light shines in the uppermost window. If you want to stop at the tower, turn to 141. If you would rather press on into town, turn to 212.

394

This Shadow Warrior carries a multitude of finely crafted daggers, slung in bandoliers across its chest. At the start of each round of combat, the Warrior throws a blade at you. Roll one die: if you roll 1–4, the dagger misses; but if you roll 5 or 6, it thuds into your flesh and you must deduct 2 points from your STAMINA. Armour or *Testing your Luck* will not reduce this damage. Whether the dagger hits you or not, you must then fight a normal Attack Round of combat.

Second SHADOW WARRIOR SKILL 9 STAMINA 9

If you defeat the Warrior, turn to 335.

395

Inside the large cavemouth, the sunlight gives way to a gentle glow – the walls are luminous. *Test your Luck*. If you are Lucky, turn to 381. If you are Unlucky, turn to 191.

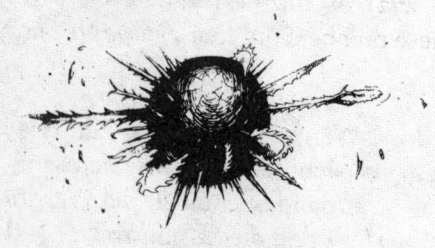

396

Roggmondo hesitates, then relaxes and says, 'All right, I believe you. I've no love for that money-grabbing ball of grease and greed either. I'll hide you – but if this is a trick and you're really working for that swine, I'll make sure you don't see the year out. If I don't get you, the Tattooists' Guild will.' He takes you to a back room, where another room is located, hidden behind a secret panel.

You spend at least an hour in here before Roggmondo tells you you can come out. Some guards *did* search the place, he tells you, but they never once suspected your presence. You thank Roggmondo and promise to return the favour one day. When you leave the tattoo parlour, Woad's men are nowhere to be seen.

If you still want to visit the east side of the market, turn to **82**; if you want to visit the west side, turn to **66**. You may not revisit a side you have already been to. When you have finished any visits, you must leave the city. Do not follow the instructions given on the market pages; instead, you must leave by either the South Gate (turn to **272**) or the nearer East Gate (turn to **60**). (Note these numbers on your *Adventure Sheet*.)

397

For a moment you stand, lost in thought, but your reverie is disturbed by a familiar voice. Though no one else seems to see it, the grass on either side of the road rustles with impressions of Jack-in-the-Green. 'This is the reward for fooling with nature. The elements have no faith in man the builder, man the user, man the destroyer, yet *you* carry tokens of worth. You are not the one to light fires, to chop down trees, to level mountains. You are good. The Earth-mother and the Horned God await you.' You are suddenly overcome by a strange dizziness. Turn to **90**.

398

'Troubled times await you,' the enigmatic figure continues, 'but the Horned God sends a gesture of goodwill: find the man of numbers, or his book. Without either, you will fail.' Then the face is gone. You decide to ally yourself with the elemental forces whom Jack-in-the-Green serves as a messenger. You will be the Earth-mother's champion against the evil Shadow Warriors.

Gornt is actually much further south than it appears on your map, and it is night-time when you finally reach the high town wall. Passing through the North Gate, you hear noises of unrest and catch the smell of smoke, yet you don't see any town guards, no gate wardens, no one at all. You are wondering what to do when you see a young man come running out of his home. He shouts, 'Go away! You're not my wife.'

A young woman comes after him. Smiling, she tugs at his wrist and says, 'But of course I'm your wife, silly. Who else could I be? Now stop being foolish and come back inside.' The man refuses, and they struggle violently.

If you want to try and put a stop to their fight, turn to **284**. If you would rather leave them alone, and make for the town centre, turn to **231**.

399

You find yourself on the Main Trade Route, far south of Cauldon Ring. Ahead, you see a number of gaily coloured carts and caravans, and a group of odd-looking folk. This is 'The Circus of Dreams', and the troupe is about to move on. It occurs to you that you could save some time on your journey by riding with them; it would also give you a chance to follow up any suspicions you may have about the circus's recent visit to Gornt. Do you want to hurry along and ask the troupe for a lift (turn to **358**) or keep your distance and continue walking alone (turn to **9**)?

400

You dodge Voivod's bone-crushing gauntlets and thrust the Spear of Doom deep into his armoured body. He cries aloud with shock, and you are flung back by an explosion of Life-force. Astonishment numbs your mind as you lie there in the dirt and witness events almost beyond your comprehension. The shambling Undead fall back into their graves, and all five Shadow Warriors reappear, only to be pulled skywards in a whirl of Life-force. The five fleeting shadows are scattered, howling on the wind, never to return. You look back towards Voivod and see that his armour has dissolved, revealing an emaciated old man. He stumbles forward crying, 'Life! I had forgotten ... The smell of the flowers, the feel of the breeze. I ... I ...'

The Sisters of Time, the Horned God and Jack-in-the-Green all appear before you. As one, they say, 'You have done well, forsaking the hand of vengeful death for that of forgiving life. By this act you have righted all the wrongs and made whole all the corruptions. Voivod, Warlord of the Apocalypse, is human once more. Take him and reacquaint him with the ways of life.' Then they are gone.

You stand there on the windswept battle plains, and put your arm round the old man who is crying with the simple joy of being alive.

FOR THE BEST IN PAPERBACKS, LOOK FOR THE

In every corner of the world, on every subject under the sun, Penguin represents quality and variety – the very best in publishing today.

For complete information about books available from Penguin – including Puffins, Penguin Classics and Arkana – and how to order them, write to us at the appropriate address below. Please note that for copyright reasons the selection of books varies from country to country.

In the United Kingdom: Please write to *Dept E.P., Penguin Books Ltd, Harmondsworth, Middlesex, UB7 0DA.*

If you have any difficulty in obtaining a title, please send your order with the correct money, plus ten per cent for postage and packaging, to *PO Box No 11, West Drayton, Middlesex*

In the United States: Please write to *Dept BA, Penguin, 299 Murray Hill Parkway, East Rutherford, New Jersey 07073*

In Canada: Please write to *Penguin Books Canada Ltd, 2801 John Street, Markham, Ontario L3R 1B4*

In Australia: Please write to the *Marketing Department, Penguin Books Australia Ltd, P.O. Box 257, Ringwood, Victoria 3134*

In New Zealand: Please write to the *Marketing Department, Penguin Books (NZ) Ltd, Private Bag, Takapuna, Auckland 9*

In India: Please write to *Penguin Overseas Ltd, 706 Eros Apartments, 56 Nehru Place, New Delhi, 110019*

In the Netherlands: Please write to *Penguin Books Netherlands B.V., Postbus 195, NL–1380AD Weesp*

In West Germany: Please write to *Penguin Books Ltd, Friedrichstrasse 10–12, D–6000 Frankfurt/Main 1*

In Spain: Please write to *Longman Penguin España, Calle San Nicolas 15, E–28013 Madrid*

In Italy: Please write to *Penguin Italia s.r.l., Via Como 4, I-20096 Pioltello (Milano)*

In France: Please write to *Penguin Books Ltd, 39 Rue de Montmorency, F-75003 Paris*

In Japan: Please write to *Longman Penguin Japan Co Ltd, Yamaguchi Building, 2–12–9 Kanda Jimbocho, Chiyoda-Ku, Tokyo 101*